UNIVERSITY OF NORTH CAROLINA
STUDIES IN THE ROMANCE LANGUAGES AND LITERATURES
Number 47

CUBA'S ROMANTIC POET
THE STORY OF PLÁCIDO

CUBA'S ROMANTIC POET
THE STORY OF PLÁCIDO

BY

FREDERICK S. STIMSON
Northwestern University

CHAPEL HILL
THE UNIVERSITY OF NORTH CAROLINA PRESS

DEPÓSITO LEGAL: V. 717. — 1964

PRINTED IN SPAIN

ARTES GRÁFICAS SOLER, S. A. — VALENCIA — 1964

To JKL, who encouraged me to write the story of Plácido.

PREFACE

Gabriel de la Concepción Valdés (1809-44), better-known by his pen name "Plácido," is now relegated to obscurity in the English-speaking world, even among specialists in Spanish American literature. In this century, Ben Frederic Carruthers' unpublished dissertation, "The Life, Work and Death of Plácido" (University of Illinois, 1941), has been the only lengthy and serious study in English of the poet. José María Heredia, Gertrudis Gómez de Avellaneda, José Martí, Julián del Casal, and Nicolás Guillén today receive most of the attention paid by North American students to Cuban bards. But the picture was different a century ago; then the press in the United States heralded the name of Plácido and publicized his story.

In Cuba, Plácido is still one of the most popular of the native poets and may well be considered the Island's outstanding romanticist. His popularity has resulted in an abundance of biographies and critical analyses of his poetic genius, both written in Spanish by Spanish American scholars, especially scholars in the "Pearl of the Antilles." Perhaps because of the plethora of these conventional approaches or by the fact that very little new data was discovered relative to the poet's life and work, other foreign writers concentrated on more unusual aspects. Much time and space have been devoted to legal documents throwing light on the trial by which Plácido lost his life, to editions of his collected works and to editorial errors, even to the authenticity of portraits purported to be of the poet, and very recently to his mistresses.

This present biography includes all these aspects of the story of Plácido; additional information is furnished by hitherto unpublished letters and documents from the New York Public Library, especially from the Wurdemann and Escoto collections of Cuban papers in the Harvard University Library, and from public and private libraries in Havana. Furthermore, this study touches upon the remaining aspects of the story, those never treated by Spanish American authorities or treated erroneously. These include the fictionized biographies listed, but never before discussed, and the lost and unpublished poems. Particularly intriguing is the tale of Plácido's popularity in the United States a century ago, as evidenced by the biographies and English translations written by North Americans.

Except for Sturgis E. Leavitt's studies bringing to light much of this material in English, it has remained buried in rare books and periodicals and has been attributed to the wrong Hispanists. In his bibliography, *Hispano-American Literature in the United States* (Cambridge, Mass., 1932), Leavitt notes the existence of this material; it is discussed at length in his "Latin-American Literature in the United States," *Revue de Littérature Comparée*, XI (1931), 126-148, an article that is unique in the field.

These nineteenth-century publications in English will interest primarily students of Anglo-Hispanic literary relations, a field of specialization somewhat neglected until the appearance of Stanley T. Williams' *The Spanish Background of American Literature* (New Haven, 1955). But they may interest others, too, because of the politico-social issues involved. Parallels become apparent between the Cuba of Plácido's era, oppressed by the tyrant Spain, and oppressed Cuba of the twentieth century. It may seem that, unfortunately, Cuban-North American political relations have improved comparatively little in over a century and that Spanish America's struggle to assume its rightful place in world affairs has been slow indeed.

Perhaps Plácido's character is more fully interpreted by viewing him through the eyes of his contemporaries in the United States as well as through those of his own people. He belonged to that group of patriot writers in Spanish America, some in the Spanish tradition of the sword and the pen, who have historical significance as well as literary. It is easy to find similarities between them and certain famous North Americans of the same romantic period: both groups belonged to the New World and watched parts of it develop from colonial outposts into proud and independent nations; many of both groups fought for the rights of man; some of both wrote stirringly, if plainly; a few in both lands were assassinated for their beliefs.

Since this period in the history of the Caribbean, with piracy, spectacular scenery, and slave trade, is as colorful and exciting as the story of the American Wild West, an attempt has been made here to sketch in some of the tropical background. The background, too, is often presented from the northern point of view, through the impressions recorded by the many visitors from the United States to the Island of Plácido's day. The list of these adventurers is a long one, containing many distinguished names; and their travel books, as well as those by nineteenth-century travelers from Europe, constitute a special, interesting field of literature in themselves.

TABLE OF CONTENTS

Chapter	Page

I. PLACIDO'S CUBA
- The colorful Caribbean 15
- Cuba and Spanish America 20
- Cuba and the United States 25

II. PLACIDO'S LIFE
- Biographies in Spanish 29
- Appearance, personality, and loves ... 32
- Childhood 44
- Youth 55
- Villa Clara 67
- Conspiracy and death 75
- North American biographies 89
- Fictional biographies 102

III. PLACIDO'S POETRY
- Poetic talent 108
- Unpublished poems 118
- North American translations 126

IV. CONCLUSION 139

SELECTED BIBLIOGRAPHY 146

Chapter I

PLACIDO'S CUBA

The colorful Caribbean

It is sometimes said that in certain ways the history of much of this world has been written in terms of a westward drive. Like the American Wild West, the Caribbean area constituted a new frontier for the adventurous. Cuba, homeland of the poet Plácido, of course formed part of this early Wild West to which by boat, instead of by wagon, fortune hunters came from Spain, France, England, and the Netherlands. Even as late as the first half of the nineteenth century, in Plácido's time, the West Indies were still witnessing a pageant as colorful as that taking place in North America when the frontier was being pushed on to California.

Color was added to the already colorful West Indian civilization by a barbarous trade which, incidentally, involved the North American government and attracted a great deal of attention in the North. This was an enterprise which began with buccaneers, was modified by privateers, and ended up as piracy, to last almost as long as the Spanish ruled in America. The heydey of piracy was over by the end of the eighteenth century, but, more modest in scope, it continued to flourish well into the nineteenth. And though originally New Providence or Nassau in the Bahamas constituted the headquarters, the "Pirate Republic," the Antilles, especially Cuba and Hispaniola, became very much involved.

So many North American vessels were pirated off the Cuban coast and elsewhere in the Caribbean in 1821 and 1822 that the United States Navy, which had been carrying on sporadic guerrilla warfare against West Indian pirates ever since the end of the War of 1812, was authorized by Congress to launch a full-fledged campaign. Support from Washington, where the Monroe Doctrine was being considered as a policy for this hemisphere, soon weakened. The task was undertaken, nevertheless, under Captain David Porter and with the cooperation of the British. The cleaning-up continued slowly and pirates were one by one rooted out of their various hideaways, including the coast of Cuba, often called "Isle of a Hundred Harbors," an ideal hideaway as this expression implies. The dogged cruising by United States patrols continued until nearly mid-century.

A description of piracy around and about Cuba, at the time when Plácido was a young man, is given by the British adventurer, Aaron Smith, who relates in the first person his trials and tribulations aboard ship seven leagues off the Island. His *Atrocities of the Pirates; being a faithful narrative of the unparalleled sufferings by the author during his captivity among the pirates of the Island of Cuba* (London, 1824), may be filled with more fancy than fact and designed, with its detailed accounts of tortures fiendishly applied by the pirates, for a more sadistic than truth-seeking public, but it is an interesting contribution to nineteenth-century travel literature. The author tells that, accused of voluntarily joining the band of Spanish and British robbers, he was tried in 1823 before the High Court of Admiralty. After recounting how he was tied to the mast, flogged, and burned by fuses, he managed to convince the Court that he was forced into the business and was acquitted.

The Island's slave trade was a matter of great concern in the United States, to abolitionists and slave traders alike. During Plácido's lifetime slavery was flourishing in both lands, to last in Cuba until 1886. Although an accurate census was probably even more difficult to obtain then than it is now in Spanish America, figures are offered by the German traveler, the statistics-obsessed Alexander Von Humboldt (1769-1859), of whom a renowned critic says, "it is impossible ... to overestimate the general currency of this traveler's writings." [1] His *The Island of Cuba*, published

---

[1] Stanley T. Williams, *The Spanish Background of American Literature* (New Haven, 1955), I, 82.

separately in English in 1856, and the Spanish version, in 1826, *Ensayo político sobre la isla de Cuba*, first appeared as Chapter XXVIII, Book X, of the chronicle, published in French in 1807 and in English in 1815, of all Humboldt's scientific expeditions in America.

According to *Island of Cuba*, in 1810 the population of Havana and suburbs alone consisted of 41,227 whites, 25,979 free colored, and 28,908 slaves. In all the "3,600 square leagues" of Cuba, the 1817 population included 290,021 whites, 115,651 free colored, and 225,268 slaves. Speaking of the total area of the Antilles, Humboldt estimated that the "blacks form nearly two-thirds of it, the whites one-sixth, and the mixed races one-seventh." Regarding the importation of Africans, he quoted the customhouse returns as showing the entrance into Havana, in 1810, of 6,672 persons; between the years 1806 and 1820, 131,829, not counting those brought illegally into other Cuban ports.

Nineteenth-century travelers differed in their opinion of the treatment this enormous number of Negroes received in Cuba. Humboldt seemed to believe that the slave in the United States fared better than the Cuban slave, but the latter better than the Jamaican slave.[2] Later in the century, other travelers, such as Richard Davey, disagreed.[3] Whether better or worse off than in the United States, the life of the Cuban slave was wretched, according to David Turnbull. Four years before Plácido's death, Turnbull wrote in his *Travels in the West. Cuba; with Notices of Porto Rico and the Slave Trade* (London, 1840):

> As the experience of years had taught me to believe that the Spaniards are a kind and warm-hearted race, and as I had frequently been told that the slave owners of the Havana were the most indulgent masters in the world, I was not a little surprised to find, as the result of personal inquiry and minute observation, that in this last particular I had been most miserably deceived, and that in no quarter, unless, perhaps, in the Brazils, which I have not visited, is the state of slavery so desperately wretched as

---

[2] *The Island of Cuba*, tr. J. S. Thrasher (New York, 1856), pp. 113, 184, 218-219, 225, 232.

[3] RICHARD DAVEY, *Cuba Past and Present* (London, 1898), p. 30.

it is at this moment on the sugar plantations of the queen of the Indies, the far-famed island of Cuba" (p. 48).

This British travel writer was the same Turnbull who was later to play an important role in Plácido's life and death. An ardent abolitionist, Turnbull visited Jamaica, center of the British slave trade, then toward the end of 1838 continued on to Cuba. Having written earlier on the French Revolution, he turned his pen toward another subject involving human liberties—slavery. He wrote a treatise on the traffic as it existed in Jamaica, then published his book on Cuba, which is filled not only with a surprising amount of apparently accurate statistics, but with an eloquent plea for manumission. At the time of its publication, he was evidently unaware that soon he would become British Consul in Havana.

Nineteenth-century travelers, even the most distinguished, seem almost to have relished describing the tortures to which Cuban slaves were subjected. Turnbull tells of the public whipping houses where lady slave owners, too delicate to witness or hear the administering of punishment at home, sent their slaves for periodic disciplining, to keep them fit, so to speak, even if they had committed no infraction. He explains that parapets were erected around these houses of correction in order to exclude from public view the streaming blood and lacerated flesh, but the parapets "totally failed in shutting in their piercing screams and piteous shrieks for mercy" (p. 53). Davey's hair-raising account of the punishment, meted daily for a week to a "handsome mulatto" who had attempted escape, concludes as follows: "They subjected him to torments too shocking for description, and rubbed his wounds with *agua ardiente*. The poor wretch, writing in agony, and shrieking with pain, was bound hand and foot to the stump of a tree." [4] This treatment was no worse, however, than that which Negroes, and perhaps some whites, were to receive in 1844. Then one of the most inhumane trials of all times took place, that of the *Conspiración de la Escalera*, as a result of which Plácido was executed.

---

[4] DAVEY, p. 30.

Although the travelers' accounts may be exaggerated and although Plácido was not a slave and only partially Negro, obviously he was ill-starred to have been born in Cuba during the first half of the nineteenth century. Much of his life must have been spent in the shadow of physical terror. Perhaps it is this terror to which he alluded, as in the following selection from the long poem "El poeta":

>Mira de allí con horror
>Este suelo engañador,
>Y advierte que es una feria
>De falsedad y miseria
>De tormento y de terror. [5]

Terror was felt not only by Negroes, however. The whites were afraid, too, and perhaps it was this fear that drove them to deal so harshly with the less fortunate race. Fear of a Negro uprising or Negro control of Cuba had been heightened by events in nearby Haiti. There the blacks, brought from Africa since early in the sixteenth century, had managed gradually to vanquish all their foes, Indian, French, English, and Spanish. By the beginning of the nineteenth century, they had abolished slavery and, in 1804, declared their independence, which France officially recognized in 1825. In creating this republic, some of the most revolting acts of atrocity were committed by both blacks and whites.

Brutality was associated with Cuba, as with Haiti, and attracted the attention of seekers of the sensational. It is interesting to note that it continued to be so even late in the century, during Cuba's fight for independence, as the almost legendary adventurer Richard Harding Davis (1846-1916) remarked in his *Cuba in War Time* (New York, 1899): "One of the questions that is most frequently asked of those who have been in Cuba is how much truth exists in the reports of Spanish butcheries. It is safe to

---

[5] *Plácido (Gabriel de la Concepción Valdés) poesías completas*, ed. Sebastián Alfredo de Morales (Havana, 1886), p. 237. Unless otherwise noted, all quotations of Plácido's verse are taken from this edition. Although Morales' syntax is questionable, an effort has been made to respect his versions, as being closest to the originals; only typographical errors have been corrected, and old-fashioned accentuation, spelling, and, occasionally, punctuation have been modernized.

answer to this that while the report of a particular atrocity may not be true, other atrocities just as horrible have occurred and nothing has been heard of them" (p. 103).

Cuba and Spanish America

Ethnologically and sociologically the Spanish West Indies formed a very distinctive corner of Latin America in the nineteenth century. In many other parts of the Spanish-speaking New World three races, the white, Negro, and Indian, fused to produce a new people. In the Caribbean area, however, the percentage of Indians was unusually low, because, as in the United States, the aboriginal civilization had been almost destroyed; the proportion of Negroes, on the other hand, was unusually large, for slaves had been imported in great number to compensate for the lack of Indian labor.

Historians are vague as to what happened to the Indians, probably originating in the Bahamas, who were living in Cuba when Columbus discovered its shores toward the end of October, 1492, and exclaimed that it was "the most beautiful land that human eyes have ever seen." [6] Apparently the natives were unable to withstand the ravages of disease and the three hundred conquistadores, who, by order of Diego de Velázquez and under the command of Pánfilo de Narváez, arrived in 1511 and within four years subjugated the Island.

Although these copper-colored, beardless Indians were tall, erect, with well-proportioned bodies, they may have been, as Dr. J. G. F. Wurdemann observed in his *Notes on Cuba* (Boston, 1844), "weak and incapable of enduring fatigue"; he spoke of them as inoffensive, docile, indolent, and negative (pp. 319, 323). This same Wurdemann was to be one of the most instrumental of the early North American travelers to Cuba to spread the story of Plácido in the United States.

---

[6] Quoted by Ben Frederic Carruthers, "The Life, Work and Death of Plácido," unpubl. diss. (University of Illinois, 1941), p. 15.

In chronicles now famous for contributing to fostering the "black legend" of Spanish cruelty in the New World, Bartolomé de las Casas gave an explanation of the Indians' fate, an explanation which probably should be taken with a grain of salt, for the well-meaning Father was inclined to exaggerate: "Murieron infinitos por hambre, fatiga, y crueles tratamientos. Otros en grande número huyeron a los montes. Muchos se ahorcaron a sí mismos; y llegaron a desear esta muerte con tantas ansias que los maridos y las mujeres formaban convenio de ahorcar primero a sus hijos por amor, después el marido a la mujer, y luego el marido a sí mismo."

In Las Casas' tract is found also the oft-repeated legend of Hatuey, the Indian chief and Cuba's first patriot hero. As the Spaniards slowly burned him to death, they attempted to convert him to Christianity. The cautious chief meditated in the flames before making any rash promises. After inquiring whether Spaniards were admitted to the Christian heaven and learning that they were, he replied that he preferred to remain pagan and go to hell. [7]

Humboldt became perplexed about the discrepancies and confusion among historians, including Las Casas, regarding the number of Cuban Indians and the facts of their destruction. Perhaps respectable chroniclers were correct in maintaining that at the time of the Island's conquest in 1511 it contained a million inhabitants, that by 1517 it contained only 14,000, and by 1553 not one Indian remained. But how could so many perish so quickly? "However active we may suppose the destructive causes to have been, the cruelty of the conquerors, the brutality of the governors, the too severe labors of the gold washings, the ravages of the small pox, and the frequency of suicide, we can hardly conceive how, in thirty or forty years, I will not say a million, but even three or four hundred thousand Indians could become entirely extinct" (pp. 234-235).

Plácido's Cuba differed from most of Spanish America in a second important way. The Island was still a Spanish colony; as

---

[7] *Colección de las obras del venerable obispo de Chiapa, Don Bartolomé de las Casas* (Paris, 1822), I, 118-120.

a Puerto Rican critic put it, Spain was continuing to "oprimir para exprimir."[8] It is to be recalled that the Spanish colonial struggle for independence was practically completed by 1826, except in the case of Cuba and Puerto Rico. At that time the new countries entered their painful period of nationalization and had to adapt themselves to a changed social and economic status. While they were embarking upon this more mature phase of development, Cuba was still in its first phase.

Cuba's colonial status meant that Plácido and his compatriots were denied a right enjoyed by citizens elsewhere in Spanish America, that of taking part in the formation of an independent country. It meant also that he lived under the old caste system which had kept Spanish America in bondage since the Conquest and which may explain in part the lack of initiative visible even today and the resultant industrial and economic backwardness. The *criollo*, the child born in the New World, was doomed to idleness or petty jobs, because important posts in Church and State went to Peninsular favorites often completely ignorant of New World needs and problems.

These conditions that had frustrated the son of a Spanish captain and an Inca Princess, the famous chronicler, El Inca Garcilaso de la Vega, three centuries before, were noted by William Cullen Bryant. Bryant, a prolific translator of Spanish poetry and the leading Hispanist in the United States until his popularity was eclipsed by that of Henry Wadsworth Longfellow, lived with Cubans in New York City, later made two trips to the Island, in 1849 and again in 1872. Quoting a friend, Bryant wrote in 1849: "[Spain's] government sends its needy nobility, and all for whom it would provide, to fill lucrative offices in Cuba — the priests, the military officers, the civil authorities, every man who fills a judicial post or holds a clerkship, is from old Spain."[9]

Turnbull noted that the "distinction of ranks among the various classes of society is as carefully kept up in Cuba as in the most aristocratical countries of the Old World" (p. 49). Wurdemann

---

[8] Eugenio María de Hostos, *Obras completas*, Vol. IX, *Temas cubanos* (Havana, 1939), 11.

[9] *Prose Writings of William Cullen Bryant*, ed. Parke Godwin (New York, 1884), II, 146.

reduced these ranks to three, the Peninsular, the creole, and the foreigner: "The native of Old Spain does not conceal his hatred of foreigners and contempt of the Creole, and shields his own inferiority of intelligence and enterprise under the cloak of hauteur... The Spaniard and the Creole thus form two distinct classes of society; and the foreigners from other countries, regarded with jealousy by one class for the liberal principles they insensibly instil in the people, and with envy by the other for dispossessing them of some of the branches of industry, constitute another class" (p. 189). He observed that the position of judge in provincial Cuban areas was, with few exceptions, extended to Peninsulars, not creoles, and that, without salary, these petty officers "like so many vultures... prey upon the unprotected within their jurisdiction" (p. 129).

At the beginning of the nineteenth century, the power which kept Cuba in bondage stemmed from the despotic Fernando VII, who, ruling in Spain from 1808 to 1833, revived the most unpleasant aspects of colonial management and sent corrupt officials to Cuba. In 1834, immediately after his reign, insular resentment became even more bitter, because, during the rule of the Queen Mother in behalf of her daughter Isabel II, one of the harshest of the Captain Generals, Miguel Tacón, was assigned to Cuba where he governed for four years.

An ultra-conservative monarchist, Tacón refused to recognize the successful revolt of Peninsular liberals in 1835, a revolt which resulted in restoring the Spanish constitution with its provision for Cuban representation on the Cortes. He was infuriated when the liberal Miguel Lorenzo, in command of the eastern part of Cuba, proclaimed this constitution in force and arranged for Cuban deputies to be sent to Spain. For a short time Islanders thought that some semblance of justice was coming their way. But Tacón overruled Lorenzo by making use of a decree of 1825 permitting the Captain General to ignore instructions from Spain, if such seemed to be to the Island's best interests. He then imprisoned or exiled some of Havana's most distinguished creoles. His highhanded action was supported in Spain, when the Cortes refused to seat Lorenzo's deputies and those from Puerto Rico.

Many stories are told about Tacón. It is related, for instance, that he allowed Havana the diversion of Italian opera because it enervated the people. But if he heard the word "liberty" sung, even if it were partially drowned out by the orchestra, he would close the theater and jail the singers, as he did when Bellini's *I Puritani* was presented. He may have known very little Italian, but he could recognize certain subversive words.[10] According to another tale — in which he is shown in a somewhat more sympathetic, an almost Solomonic, light — he acted as judge at the trial of a dissipated count who had abducted a beautiful peasant girl. Her fiancé protested, but Tacón decided the case in favor of the count and ordered him to marry the girl at that very moment. Upon returning alone to his plantation, the count was murdered by Tacón's henchmen. Thus the peasant could marry her fiancé and at the same time inherit the count's estate.[11]

After Tacón's severe rule ended in 1838, the weak Gerónimo Valdés took over, to be followed five years later by Leopoldo O'Donnell, who, in harshness, outdid even Tacón. O'Donnell's cruelty was to reach its climax during the trial of the *Conspiración de la Escalera*.

Some historians maintain that Cuba made only a halfhearted attempt to follow the example of the other Spanish countries in the New World. In comparison with them, perhaps, Cuba did not have a grievous complaint against the Peninsula. In matters of trade, the Crown permitted the wealthy "Pearl of the Antilles" certain advantages not altogether sanctioned by law. And Cubans were leary of Simón Bolívar's interest in freeing them and also their slaves; with a population of over half Negro, there was the threat that emancipation might be accompanied by a Negro insurrection.

Naturally some echo of Spanish America's cries for freedom reached the Island. But the secret societies of liberation, such as the famous *Soles y Rayos de Bolívar*, were quickly suppressed. Not until the middle of the century, a few years after Plácido's death, did any serious, concerted effort to overthrow the rule of

---

[10] Hostos, pp. 12-13.
[11] Charles E. Chapman, *A History of the Cuban Republic* (New York, 1927), pp. 32-33.

the mother country take place; then, between 1848 and 1851, the Venezuelan General Narciso López undertook unsuccessful expeditions of liberation. In the latter year Spanish authorities caught and executed him.

Cuba and the United States

Cuba's romantic appeal to North Americans of the first half of the past century is well-illustrated by the following description included in what was probably the first survey of Spanish American poetry every printed in the United States, "The Poetry of Spanish America." [12] This article appeared in one of the most distinguished of the early journals, *The North American Review* (LXVIII [1849], 129-160). "Passing eastward across the Gulf, our eyes rest on the Queen of the Antilles, on fair and glorious Cuba, that 'summer isle of Eden,' whose name fills the mind with the most enchanting pictures of tropical beauty, the most delicious dreams of splendor and luxury and magnificent ease, — that garden of the West, gorgeous with perpetual flowers and brilliant with the plumage of innumerable birds, beneath whose glowing sky the teeming earth yields easy and abundant harvest to the toil of man, and whose capacious harbours invite the commerce of the world" (p. 137). So enthused one of the most active but now most forgotten early Hispanists, William Henry Hurlbert, who was also one of the first of Plácido's biographers.

The same year Bryant wrote the following pleasant account of Cuba's capital: "The city of Havana has a cheerful appearance, seen from the harbor. Its massive houses, built for the most part of the porous rock of the island, are covered with stucco, generally of a white or cream color, but often stained sky-blue or bright yellow. Above these rise the dark towers and domes of the churches, apparently built of a more durable material, and looking

---

[12] An exhaustive list of the later accounts, written in the United States, of Spanish American literature is given in Sturgis E. Leavitt's "Latin-American Literature in the United States," *Revue de Littérature Comparée*, XI (1931), 126-148.

more venerable for the gay color of the dwellings amid which they stand" (p. 120).

Apparently it was the bright color in Havana which especially appealed to North American romantics. The author, lawyer, sailor, and humanitarian, Richard Henry Dana, Jr. (1815-82), in *To Cuba and Back* (Boston, 1859), also commented on the delightful colors he saw as his boat docked: "We are to go in at sunrise, and few, if any, are the passengers that are not on deck at the first glow of dawn... The steep Morro, with its tall sentinel lighthouse, and its towers and signal staffs and teeth of guns, is coming out into clear daylight; the red and yellow striped flag of Spain — blood and gold — floats over it. Point after point in the city becomes visible; the blue and white and yellow houses, with their roofs of dull red tiles, the quaint old Cathedral towers, and the almost endless lines of fortifications" (p. 29).

North Americans over a century ago were enraptured by Cuba's tropical beauty, as well as intrigued by the sinister mystery of piracy, the slave trade, and atrocity.[13] The eccentric James Gates Percival, for instance, in his poem "Apostrophe to the Island of Cuba" (1822), damned the region as an outpost of slavery and slaughter. Some of the more adventurous authors, such as Philip Freneau, North America's leading eighteenth-century poet, traveled through the West Indies; Edward Coote Pinckney, a somewhat less celebrated poet, went there as a midshipman, around 1820; Epes Sargent reached Cuba in 1835. Some early writers even resided in Cuba; inheriting a Cuban plantation, the strange poetess, Maria Gowen Brooks, settled there to write her best-known work, *Zophiël* (1829).

Early novelists made use of the West Indies, especially Cuba, as a backdrop for adventure stories. Whether or not they possessed firsthand knowledge of the area was a matter of little consequence; with a setting of tropical islands, their dime novels were assured of success. A passing use of such a background is made in *Constantia Neville; or, the West Indian* (1800), for instance, by Helena Wells, who published her novels in London. Interest

---

[13] See my brief discussion of Cuban influence on early North American fiction, *Orígenes del hispanismo norteamericano* (Mexico, 1961), pp. 87-97.

in atrocity is seen in Mary Hassal's *Secret History; or, the Horrors of St. Domingo* (Philadelphia, 1808). Typical of the fiction dealing with Caribbean pirates is the series of works on the French corsair, Jean Lafitte. The best-known novel on this subject is Joseph Holt Ingraham's *Lafitte: The Pirate of the Gulf*, published in 1836, although an anonymous version was published earlier, probably in 1825.[14] Another tale of pirates is *Ramon, the Rover of Cuba* (Boston, 1829), also published anonymously.

In this adventure fiction, comments concerning Cubans are flattering and reveal North America's sympathy for the Island. In *Ramon*, for instance, the author wrote: "The poorest Montero of Cuba or the common sailor of a Spanish man of war has a sense of honour, which he is ever ready to vindicate with his blood" (p. viii). In a more serious work, "A Story of Cuba," Bryant said in 1828: "Of all the citizens of Spanish America, I believe them to possess the best character" (I, 263).

The romantic drive was not the only motivation for northern interest in Cuba during the first half of the past century. One historian alluded to another when he wrote, "Cuba's troubles, with their political implications... furnished a topic for the magazines."[15] Political matters have always kept the two countries in close contact.

Many vied for Cuban favor, among them the British who had captured the Island from Spain in 1762, but had returned it a year later. As early as 1807 Thomas Jefferson toyed with the idea of annexation; the idea seemed especially good when Napoleon crossed the Pyrenees the following year and claimed the right to rule Spanish America. During the second two decades of the century, the United States continued to fear either British or French occupation. In 1823 and 1824 Colombia and Mexico proposed to set the Island free. From that point on until the Spanish American War, the United States encouraged Spain to hold on to her colony rather than cede it to a foreign power.

---

[14] See G. H. Orians, "Lafitte: A Bibliographical Note," *American Literature*, IX (1937), 351-353.

[15] Frank Luther Mott, *A History of American Magazines*, Vol. I, 1741-1850 (New York, 1930), 465.

Evidences of the close political tie between the United States and Cuba were the filibustering expeditions organized in the North, while conspiracies were being plotted in Havana. Upon the failure of an insurrection, writers like José María Heredia (1803-39) and José Martí (1853-95) sought asylum in New York, where they worked for the cause of liberty. Some North American sympathizers and some Cubans — including the distinguished historian of slavery, José Antonio Saco (1797-1879), himself once banished by Tacón — favored the idea of annexing Cuba to the United States.

A third reason for northern interest in Cuba was, of course, trade. The Island was coveted not only for its strategic location, but for its produce, especially sugar and tobacco, and, in Plácido's time, slaves. According to Wurdemann's figures, "during the years 1840, 1841, and 1842, we exported to Cuba articles valued at $18,166,428. Our imports during these three years, amounted to $34,202,347 from Cuba" (p. 246). Reasonably correct and revealing statistics concerning Cuban trade with the United States during the early nineteenth century are to be found in the charts of the historian, or, more properly speaking, statistician, Ramón de la Sagra, author of *Historia económico-política y estadística de la Isla de Cuba* (Havana, 1831).

One of the most interesting manifestations of the early tie between the two countries is the work published by North Americans on the subject of Plácido. In the nineteenth century his name evoked in the United States some of the same sympathy and emotion that it still does in Cuba. This emotion, amounting almost to worship, is visible in the following passage from the introduction to an outstanding biography published in Havana: "Es una página muy triste, es una historia de lágrimas y duelo la que vamos a presentar al lector: la vida y muerte de Plácido, la mancha más negra de nuestra historia política y literaria, el baldón más ignominioso que puede echarse en cara a las instituciones y a la tiranía de otros tiempos." [16]

---

[16] Francisco Calcagno, *Poetas de color* (Havana, 1878), p. 5.

Chapter II

PLACIDO'S LIFE

Biographies in Spanish

Although Plácido's life was short — thirty-five years — many essential details of it are missing. And much of what is not missing, what is now accepted as fact, is undocumented and may well be legend rather than truth. The so-called facts come from four sources, two of which might be considered primary. The latter comprise the biographies written by the poet's contemporaries in Cuba and a handful of legal documents which have come to light. A third source, not the least interesting, consists of nineteenth-century biographical sketches published in English in North American journals. The last source is that of the twentieth-century biographies written by Spanish Americans. In the main, these modern authors assort, assemble, and interpret facts taken from the earlier accounts; they attempt to paint a more complete picture, but often do so with the aid not of additional documentation, very little of which has appeared this century, but with that of additional imagination.

The first of the nineteenth-century accounts in Spanish, an undistinguished one, was included in the 1856 (New York) anthology of Plácido's verse compiled by an admirer of the poet, Francisco Javier Vingut, who had, in each of the two previous years, published similar, though less complete, collections. Vingut, born in Trinidad, was a journalist in Washington, D. C., a teacher of foreign languages in New York City, and the editor of Saco's works. An inaccurate biography of 1863 should be noted, as the next to be published. Although in French, not Spanish, it is often referred to by Spanish American critics. It was included in a preface by Louis Jourdan to a Parisian collection of French translations poorly fashioned by a certain D. Fontaine. Jourdan lived in Cuba from 1839 until 1848 where presumably he became interested in Plácido.

In 1872 Eugenio María Hostos, Puerto Rico's outstanding literary critic, sociologist, and champion of West Indian freedom from Spain, published his *Biografía de Plácido* (Santiago de Chile). Pedro José Guiteras' biographical sketch of the poet appeared in the newspaper *El Mundo Nuevo* (1874), printed in New York. Guiteras was a distinguished scholar who had worked for the cause of female education in Cuba, then retired to New York to write a history of his native land. Another important contribution, with respect to new data, foreign interest in Plácido, and the bloody political background, was given by the lexicographer Francisco Calcagno, in his *Poetas de color* (Havana, 1878) and more briefly in his *Diccionario biográfico cubano* (Havana) of the same year. A biography, concerned primarily with denying Plácido's complicity in the *Conspiración de la Escalera*, was published in Cuba's leading journal, the *Revista Cubana* (1885), by one of the few Cuban scholars whose name is well-known outside the Island, Antonio Bachiller y Morales, lawyer, professor, writer, editor, and public figure, who, like Guiteras, resided for a time in New York.

The biography included in *Plácido (Gabriel de la Concepción Valdés) Poesías completas* (Havana, 1886), is indispensable, as one critic observes, because it was written by one of the few biographers who knew the poet intimately.[17] Sebastián Alfredo de Morales, the "Lince" referred to in Plácido's verse, was probably the poet's best friend. Morales remained loyal to Plácido to the bitter end and visited him in the Matanzas prison. Because of this friendship, Morales had to flee Cuba after the poet's execution. A naturalist concerned with the study of Cuban flora, Morales was also chief editor of the provincial newspaper *La Aurora de Matanzas*, when Plácido copiously contributed verse to it.

---

[17] CARRUTHERS, p. 2.

Morales' collection was the first and only large edition of Plácido's poetry and is by far the most complete. It comes closest to being the definitive edition, but it has been criticized because some of the poorest works are included and some of the best are omitted; Morales has been bitterly attacked for over-editing with changes and even additions, for his interpretation of the word *inédito,* for artificial classifications, and sundry other matters.

Manuel Sanguily, an opponent of the "sacred cows of literature," as one authority puts it, [18] published a biography and a "debunking" of Plácido in *Hojas Literarias* (Havana, 1894). This sensational study criticizes the veneration in which the poet has been held and questions the authenticity of some of his best-known works, those written just before execution. Of Franco-British parentage, Sanguily was at one time Cuban Secretary of State and spent considerable time in Europe and the United States campaigning for Cuban independence.

The one remaining great nineteenth-century work on Plácido is that by the celebrated Spanish critic, Marcelino Menéndez y Pelayo. His *Historia de la poesía hispanoamericana* (Madrid, 1894), was commissioned by the Royal Spanish Academy; later included in the *Antología de poetas hispano-americanos* (Madrid, 1927), it contains more stylistic critique than biography, and partially refutes the caustic comments that the same author, apparently somewhat casually, made about Plácido in his earlier *Horacio en España* (Madrid, 1885).

The second of the primary sources includes the documents which have come to light; most of these were first reproduced in the twentieth-century biographies of Domingo Figarola-Caneda, García Garófalo Mesa, and recently, Leopoldo Horrego Estuch. Important are the birth and marriage certificates, the last will and testament, letters, and reports from authorities in the Spanish colonial government.

With respect to the twentieth-century biographies, the earliest appeared in *Biografías americanas* (París, 1906), by Enrique Piñeyro, one of the most eminent of all Cuban scholars. But the most unusual is *Plácido (poeta cubano),* published in Havana in

---

[18] CARRUTHERS, p. 3.

1922 by Figarola-Caneda, the Island's painstaking and outspoken critic. His meticulous, at times almost picayune, approach to problems is exemplified by his careful analyses of the arguments concerning an authentic portrait of Plácido, concerning the details of Heredia's visit to Matanzas, and the supposed attack in poetry on Plácido by José Jacinto Milanés. It is exemplified also by his denunciation of Morales on the aforementioned counts; this denunciation is documented with quotations from others who shared the same opinion of Morales, in particular, Enrique José Varona (1849-1933), the poet who became vice president of the Cuban Republic.

Two selected anthologies have appeared, prepared by Eligio de la Puente (Havana, 1930) and Jorge Casals (Havana, 1944), each containing biographical sketches. *Plácido, poeta y mártir* (Mexico, 1938), by Garófalo Mesa, a critic as well-known in Mexico as in his native Cuba, contains reproductions of legal papers showing the unrest in Cuba in 1844 and the fear of a Negro uprising. The two most recent biographies have been those by Horrego Estuch and Itzhak Bar-Lewaw. The former brought out in Havana two editions (1944, 1949) of his *Plácido, el poeta infortunado;* his latest work (1960), with the same title, is said to include new material, but as is too often the case with biographies of Plácido, little documentation is produced to substantiate the claims. In *Plácido, vida y obra* (Mexico, 1960), Bar-Lewaw's interpretation of various matters is very similar to that of Calcagno and Horrego Estuch, and he unquestioningly repeats the same old errors regarding English translations.

Appearance, Personality, and Loves

Almost everything that has to do with Plácido, even portraits of him, is clouded with uncertainty. In the lengthy discussion by Figarola-Caneda of the authenticity of surviving likenesses, the field is narrowed down to two. One is the portrait supposedly copied from a drawing found in the papers of a certain Pío Dubrocq in Matanzas and subsequently published in *Album para Todos* (Havana, 1885); in this the poet is shown with a plump face and large eyes. The second is a crayon sketch by a Rojas from Cádiz or Seville, a sketch owned by Morales and published in his anthology of 1886; in this Plácido looks emaciated and has small eyes. Both portraits are the smooth and fatuous type popular a century ago, with all facial lines removed. Poorly copied from an original or from somebody's memory, they are indistinct and unpleasant. But one or both are reproduced in most of the twentieth-century biographies.

Often told is the story that in 1836 an attempt was made to publish a collection of Plácido's verse with a lithograph of the author. Friends begged him to pose for the picture in elegant attire, like a "real poet," but Plácido insisted on dressing as he did when pursuing his vocation, which was not composing poetry, but rather carving tortoise-shell combs which formed a part of ladies' elaborate coiffures. At such times he was bareheaded and wore a wide-collared shirt open low at the neck. Perhaps his friends thought he might at least "dress up," which he did on special occasions by wearing, in addition, a straw hat, a black ribbon bow tie, and, if finances permitted, gold shoe buckles. But when the project to publish the collection was abruptly abandoned, apparently so was the project to preserve Plácido's appearance for posterity. Although some admirers maintained that the lithograph was finished, Morales insisted that it was not, that Plácido's wife confirmed it was not, and that the only authentic likeness was the sketch by Rojas.

It is to be hoped that Morales' verbal portrait is more accurate and revealing than the blurred crayon sketch. According to the former, almost amusing in its detail, Plácido was thin, of medium height. His skin was smooth, not hairy, and his complexion was light. His well-shaped head was crowned with curly rather than kinky hair; the forehead was high; the face, oval, with thick, slanting eyebrows; his eyes were small, black, and lively; his nose, aquiline; his mouth was sensitive, and the lips, thin; his teeth were small, white, and even; his expression was friendly and boyish, sometimes bold, sometimes melancholy. His bearing and stride were free and easy. His voice was silvery, eloquent, and decisive. All in all, he had that "tono levantado que revela el genio y nos le hace distinguir al primer golpe de vista" (p. xxiv).

Guiteras agreed that Plácido had an enviable physique and bearing, but observed that his face was darkened by a thin beard. Hostos described the poet, or rather some portrait of him, in a rather ethnological way, to show what was inherited from his colored father and what from his white mother: "El cabello rebelde, el pómulo saliente, el brillo característico del ojo, denuncian en aquella fisonomía al africano, en tanto que el ángulo facial, la regularidad de la nariz, la delgadez de los labios, la extensión de la frente, delatan al blanco" (p. 14). Hostos differed from Morales in saying that Plácido's eyes were very large—as they are shown in the Dubrocq portrait. Large or small eyes, the concensus was that Plácido was a handsome young man.

Was Plácido's personality equally attractive? With respect to his personality as a child, Morales referred to him as *travieso*. The only biographer to shed much light on the boy Plácido was Guiteras, although his remarks on this score have been appropriated, without acknowledgment, by various twentieth-century critics. Guiteras reported that as a child the poet was proud and aggressive, more than holding his own with his comrades; in fact, he became the leader of his "gang" and, as such, wore a red ribbon across his chest; fearlessly he led his playmates into fights and skirmishes. He became an excellent swimmer; he loved this sport to the extent that occasionally he cut school to indulge in it. Guiteras, rather wistfully it might seem, thereby tried to compare his hero with another romantic poet, Lord Byron, and suggested that, in the field of swimming at least, the Cuban excelled his English counterpart.

Concerning Plácido's adult personality, biographers, supported by little or no documentation, unquestioningly assume that his pen name was apt. Perhaps the writer who knew him best, Morales, is to be believed, but obviously Morales was inclined to idealize his friend. According to him, Plácido was polite and modest, as if always aware of his low social position. In arguments he never raised his voice, even if he were clearly in the right. He loved solitude and the countryside: "Muchas veces le sorprendí vagaroso en los sitios más agrestes del Yumurí, o reclinado sobre alguna peña pasando horas enteras sin mudar de actitud" (p. xxiv). Guiteras maintained that Plácido's disposition was friendly, happy, and affectionate. As far as religion was concerned, he was devout, without being fanatic. And he had a prodigious memory, recited beautifully, and possessed a marvelous ability to improvise verse.

With respect to financial matters, Plácido was apparently too generous. The same critic said that the poet would lend money, even when he was in need himself, and that once Plácido remarked that he wished to possess "inagotables riquezas para no oír las quejas de la humanidad sin aliviarlas" (January, 15, p. 22). According to Morales, if Plácido were ever in debt, it was not from squandering money on vices, for he had none. This biographer added, incidentally, that in those days Cubans could be jailed for debts, a law that if it had not been repealed, would have resulted in the imprisonment of half the Island's population.

Morales proudly observed that Plácido never drank liquor; he never improvised with anything but beer, his favorite drink; he even refused wine with meals. Then the same biographer reproduced verbatim, as if a stenographer had been present, the poet's remarks while walking through the woods of the Yumurí: "He sido muy desgraciado desde la cuna; a veces creo en la estrella aciaga que nos persigue hasta la tumba. Creo que si no tuviese yo una cabeza tan débil para la bebida habría más de una vez apagado los gritos de mis infortunios con la embriaguez; pero ni aun esto me es dado, pues mi cerebro es tan débil que una gota de alcohol me trastorna hasta el extremo de no dejarme mover; además, yo aborrezco la embriaguez y no creo que ella sería un refugio para mis desgracias." Morales concluded: "Asevero muy solemnemente que Plácido jamás se embriagó, que no era bebedor y que sus costumbres nada tenían de licenciosas" (p. xx).

Since most of the data concerning Plácido is contradictory, it is no surprise that, regarding the poet's temperament, others disagreed with Morales and Guiteras, the poet's two staunchest defenders and perhaps most knowledgeable of the early biographers. Hostos, for instance, believed that Plácido was not as even-tempered and kind as legend had it and asserted that in New York some of the latter's friends said that he "tenía llenos de ironía los labios y su lengua era una daga" (p. 34). Calcagno angrily denied that Plácido was a "mulato pendenciero, borrachón y disoluto en todos los terrenos donde se le presentaba la ocasión," as some unidentified writer had maintained (*Poetas de color*, p. 15). In a curious biography published in a Madrid journal the year of Plácido's death, *Revista de Teatros* (September 23), an "F. U." observed that the "cánticos puros de su lira se apagaron entre los vicios de un torpe sensualismo," when he was "entregado al vino y a las mujeres."

Critics who thus appraise Plácido's character might point to poems like the following as revelatory of an innate sensualism and viciousness:

LOS TRES ANATEMAS

¡Maldito una y mil veces el instante
En que te vi, mujer, mujer impía!
Y encendí, sin temer tu alevosía,
La llama fiel de mi pasión constante.
 ¿Forcé yo acaso, hiena devorante,
Tu voluntad infiel que fuese mía?
¿Por qué, alma dura, corazón de harpía,
Robaste mi quietud, pérfida amante?
 Cérquente, cruel, las sombras aflictivas
Con que has nublado mi apacible estrella,
Y en premio a tu maldad, de Dios recibas:
Que jamás te oigas alabar de bella,
Que treinta lustros sin amores vivas,
Y que te lleven a enterrar doncella. (p. 9)

Apparently in the eyes of Cuban biographers at least, a strong sexual drive is an admirable attribute in a poet. Thus, few writers attempt to minimize Plácido's amorous prowess. Horrego Estuch seems to have hit the jackpot, so to speak, in his latest version of *Plácido, el poeta infortunado*, by detecting in the poet's work evidence of at least five major love affairs. And, introducing the subject with the cliché that by definition all poets are romantically inclined, the same critic almost proudly observes that his hero covered the color scale from white to bronze to black. In his recent biography, Bar-Lewaw discusses the same five affairs; he introduces the subject by remarking that the "cálida tierra cubana y su ardiente sol tropical agitan prematuramente las pasiones de la juventud," and Plácido's were no exception (p. 37).

With little proof other than the celebrated romance "La flor de la cera," biographers maintain that Plácido's first great romance was with a beautiful and wealthy girl from Matanzas, when he was twenty years old. Since she had white skin (though perhaps she was a mulatto) and was vain and arrogant, the affair was doomed from the beginning. The most dramatic account of it is Hostos': "Era poeta, y amaba lo bello que veía. Vió lo bello, y lo amó. Era una mujer blanca: él era pardo; una hija de la fortuna: él un bastardo" (p. 17). In the following selection Plácido refers to the girl as "Lesbia" and to himself as "Delio":

>   Una mañana de abril,
> Antes que el alba serena
> Ornara el cielo de nácar
> Y los pensiles de perlas,
>   Paseaba yo divertido
> Del San Juan por la ribera,
> En un jardín que a su orilla
> Preciosas plantas ostenta.
>   Con un cestillo de mimbre
> Y unas tijerillas nuevas,
> Estaba una joven linda
> Cortando "flores de cera."
>   Ocultéme entre unas ramas
> De jasmín y madreselva,
> Que abrazan a un rojo Adonis
> Formando bóveda espesa...
>   Hablando consigo misma,
> De que la oyesen ajena,
> Tomando la más lozana
> Dijo la simple doncella:
>   —Dice bien Delio, que eres
> De los jardines la reina.
> ¡Si yo fuese tan hermosa
> Como "la flor de la cera!"
>   De su voz el eco suave
> Me hizo conocer a Lesbia,
> Con la cual bailé mil veces
> De Pueblo Nuevo en las fiestas;
>   Y de Delio bajo el nombre
> La hice amorosas protestas:
> ¡Conque aquí mi Lesbia mora
> Y de su Delio se acuerda!
>   ¿Podré dudar que me ama

Esta inocente belleza,
Tan alegre y tan sencilla
Como "la flor de la cera?"...
   Fuése a orillas de un estanque
De agua clara, limpia y tersa;
Vióse el rostro en el cristal
Y exclamó de gozo llena:
   —Ya estará Delio en el puente,
Y cuando pasar me vea
Dirá que voy tan preciosa
Como "la flor de la cera."   (pp. 308-310)

"Lesbia" is said to have been the subject also of the following erotic sonnet in which Plácido, disillusioned and embittered, sarcastially questions her fidelity, although possibly their love was never consummated.

A MI AMADA

Mira, mi bien, cuán mustia y deshojada
Está con el calor aquella rosa
Que ayer, brillante, fresca y olorosa
Puse en tu blanca mano perfumada.
   Dentro de poco tornaráse en nada:
No verás en el mundo alguna cosa
Que a mudanza feliz o dolorosa
No se encuentre sujeta y obligada.
   Sigue a las tempestades la bonanza
Síguenle al gusto el tedio y la tristeza;
Mas perdona que tengo desconfianza
   Y dude de tu amor y tu terneza,
Que habiendo en todo el mundo tal mudanza
¿Sólo en tu corazón habrá firmeza?   (p. 4)

Horrego Estuch points to the bronze-skinned "Filena," as Plácido called a certain María Josefa, as the second great love. The poet is supposed to have met her on one of his frequent trips from Matanzas to Havana. On a subsequent trip he learned that she had not only forgotten him, but was having an affair. Although Horrego Estuch believes that Plácido was so disillusioned that suicide was contemplated, it seems more likely that the threats of suicide followed the tragedy of Plácido's third love, Rafaela.

With this third romance, the best documented, critics have had a field day, Carruthers calling it the "really great love affair of Plácido's life" (p. 23). The early biographers, Morales and Guiteras, relate that Rafaela and her mother were slaves on the estate in Matanzas of an aristocratic white woman. Childless, this interesting woman treated Rafaela as she would her own daughter; at the mother's request, she had Rafaela baptized and freed. She treated her slaves kindly; an abolitionist, she would have enjoyed freeing all of them, but was prevented by the fear of the suspicion and enmity such a move would have caused among the planters. Instead, she offered many colored people refuge and sanctuary in her home.

From white to bronze, then to black, Plácido had indeed run the gamut of color. Now his search was ended. He planned to marry this girl, "Fela" or "Zelmira" as he called her in verse, despite his father's objections to her color. (As Guiteras pointed out, considerable class distinction, based on shade of skin, existed among the Negroes of Cuba.) A second drawback was the fact that she had a second suitor, a certain Pilar González, whom she persisted in seeing even after Plácido began his courtship. To compensate for her dark color and unfaithfulness, however, she had an education; at least she could read and write, play the harp and piano, sing, paint, and embroider. Furthermore, she was so beautiful as to be called the "Ethiopian Venus."

The marriage never took place, because Rafaela was caught in the cholera epidemic sweeping over Havana in 1833, a tragic event about which Plácido wrote a long elegy. In one stanza he observed that this epidemic, which must have assumed the proportions of a medieval plague, was as voracious as war:

EL CÓLERA EN LA HABANA

No se diga que el rayo de la guerra
Es más voraz que el abrasante azote
Del Cólera feroz. Cuando se cierra
El paso a un batallón por muchos miles
Fuertes guerreros del opuesto bando,
Dádoles es para salvar las vidas,
Rendir sus armas o morir matando;
Más con este cometa que se lanza
De la infernal región, envuelto en muerte,
Morir y ver morir ¡oh cruda suerte!
Es la única y bárbara esperanza.   (p. 537)

The sound of the wagons, hauling the dead to the cemeteries, was a sound that Plácido was not soon to forget:

> Aun están en mi oído resonando
> De los fúnebres carros
> Las terríficas ruedas,
> Que conducen por plazas y alamedas
> Los recientes cadáveres del Cólera,
> Y oigo el adusto conductor que canta,
> Por ver, buscando calma a su tormento,
> Si de valor con el fingido acento
> El torvo ceño de la muerte espanta.   (pp. 537-538)

Critics fairly rhapsodize over Plácido's grief upon Rafaela's sudden death. Some say that his only chance for happiness, solace, and refuge from the cruel outside world seemed lost forever. Carruthers dramatically observes that in the "true romantic tradition Plácido had suffered the blow which was to make him a great poet. As Lamartine grieved for the dead Elvira, Musset for the inconstant George Sand, so Plácido wept for his lost Fela. For a time he fell so ill his own life was despaired of" (p. 24). In his will he left an embrace to her as well as to his wife. Poem after poem touches on this his great loss. Of these works, some critics consider the following sonnet the most moving:

A ELINO, EN LA MUERTE DE FELA

> Ven, Elino, a llorar; ya murió Fela;
> Y acabó para siempre mi ventura,
> Y yo expiro de pena y de amargura
> Si tu tierna amistad no me consuela.
>   ¡Ay! cómo el tiempo de la dicha vuela;
> Rayo parece que el pesar augura,
> Hollando el paso de su planta dura
> Cuanto se guarda con mayor cautela.
>   Yo no puedo vivir sin ser amado,
> Ni espero más amar, ni ser querido:
> Moriré triste de dolor postrado;
>   Pero antes quiero por tu fe traído
> Un fúnebre ciprés dejar plantado
> Sobre la tumba de mi bien perdido.   (p. 7)

In the romantic fashion, Plácido swore eternal love:

> La pasión que le juré
> Y que si por mi mal vivo mil años
> Mil años su memoria guardaré. [19]

And in the last stanza of the sonnet, "A mi amigo Nicolás Ayala, en la muerte de Fela," Plácido suggested that only death would free him from grief:

> Mi terrible aflicción y pena fuerte
> Por mi perdido bien que adoré tanto,
> Sólo puede aliviarse con la muerte.   (p. 5)

"A una ingrata" was once considered another sonnet resulting from the end of the romance with "Lesbia." The modern authority on Plácido's love life, Horrego Estuch, however, takes the work as evidence that in 1836 the poet fell in love again (apparently despite his memories of Fela). The girl referred to here, "Celia," was, like "Lesbia," white, beautiful, and "frigid," and the affair, like that with "Lesbia," was short-lived. Perhaps there was a difference, though; it is thought that this later love was definitely consummated.

> Basta de amor: si un tiempo te quería
> Ya se acabó mi juvenil locura,
> Porque es, Celia, tu cándida hermosura
> Como la nieve, deslumbrante y fría.
>   No encuentro en ti la extrema simpatía
> Que mi alma ardiente contemplar procura,
> Ni entre las sombras de la noche oscura,
> Ni a la espléndida faz del claro día.
>   Amor no quiero como tú me amas,
> Sorda a los ayes, insensible al ruego;
> Quiero de mirtos adornar con ramas
>   Un corazón que me idolatre ciego
> Quiero besar a una deidad de llamas,
> Quiero abrazar a una mujer de fuego.   (p. 4)

---

[19] Quoted by Hostos, p. 49; by Guillermo Rivera, "El ensayo de Hostos sobre Plácido," *Hispania*, XXII (1939), 146; and by others.

The romance was doomed for more reasons than frigidity and difference in skin color, however. According to the following lines, "Celia" was not only having an affair with another lover, as had Filena, but was trying to force Plácido to accept, as his own, the child resulting from the other union.

> Te consagré mi amor constante y fino
> Entonces nos juramos mutuamente
> Sernos fieles y bien te lo he cumplido.
> No así tú, que perjura y alevosa,
> Pagas traidoramente mi cariño;
> Dasme un rival y con doblada astucia
> Para colmo final del homicidio,
> El triste fruto que en tu seno alientas
> Quieres le reconozca por mi hijo.
> Así lo hiciera, cuando pruebas claras
> No tuviera, infeliz, de sus designios;
> Pero ya cerciorado de tu infamia,
> Ya que conozco tu fingir inicuo,
> Y el arte veo con que eludir quieres
> Las palpables verdades que no he visto.
> (*Horrego Estuch* [1960], p. 50)

Plácido's fifth and supposedly last encounter with the opposite sex is documented by a marriage certificate, filed in the Church Registry of San Carlos de Matanzas and reproduced in various of the later biographies.[20] According to it, on November 27, 1842, in Matanzas, Plácido, "natural de la Real Casa Cuna de la Habana," married the legitimate María Gila Ramona Morales y Poveda. The biographer Morales provided the information that her parents were freeborn; the father, Doroteo, a tailor and musician; Pilar, a midwife. Perhaps Plácido had been visiting their home as early as 1839, where he had been treated as one of the family. As to further details, critics differ. Some say Gila was mulatto, but the dependable writer, Piñeyro, maintained that she was of "pura sangre africana," just like Rafaela (p. 345).

Apparently the marriage was merely a convenience, perhaps a result of Plácido's affection for the entire family, especially the

---

[20] See CARRUTHERS, p. 62; LEOPOLDO HORREGO ESTUCH, *Plácido, el poeta infortunado* (Havana, 1960), pp. 331-332; GARCÍA GARÓFALO MESA, *Plácido, poeta y mártir* (Mexico, 1938), pp. 95-96; and others.

mother. The convenience was not of the financial kind, however, to judge from one of the few preserved items of the poet's correspondence, a letter dated November 11, 1942, that is, about two weeks before the wedding. Sent from the "Palacio de las Necesidades" to a friend identified only as "P. D.," it is amusing and pathetic at the same time: "Muy Sr. mío: Hallándome poéticamente enfermo y no siéndome posible convertir los sonetos y letrillas en sustancias alimenticias, me veo en la necesidad de ... suplicar a usted no deje de socorrer en algo a este pobre diablo, que por andarse haciendo moriquetas a las Musas se halla hoy en cruz y en cuadro y sitiado del hambre, que es el enemigo más encarnizado y terrible de este su atento servidor" (Guiteras, January 15, p. 22).

Perhaps the delights of marriage, or of a marriage of convenience, were ephemeral. Perhaps, as Morales explained it, the comb business fell off, and the young husband had to search elsewhere for work. At any rate, a little more than three months after the ceremony, Plácido left his wife at home in Matanzas, presumably without any support, and proceeded into the interior of Cuba. Later, Gila, when a childless widow, was to marry again—this time a survivor of the *Conspiración de la Escalera,* a certain Secundino Arango.

Plácido's opinion of matrimony, as seen in his poetry, was somewhat baleful. In the following selection from the well-known ballad "Ya me caso," he reluctantly and ironically decides he may join the "guild" of the married; the picture of the life his wife would lead is bleak indeed:

> Antes era yo enemigo
> Terrible del casamiento;
> Mas como dice el refrán
> Que "todo lo acaba el tiempo."
>   Con los años voy por grados
> De mi oposición cediendo,
> Y estoy medio convertido
> A ser un socio del gremio.
>   —¡Qué diablos! (suelo decirme)
> Si me caso nada pierdo;
> Cuando estoy rico, me faltan
> Siete reales para un peso...

> En fin, se es tan arreglada
> Que no le gusten paseos,
> Que lave la ropa, cosa,
> Y que cocine (en habiendo).
>   Que se nutra de quintillas,
> Se vista de diarios viejos,
> Y saboree las frutas
> Que yo le pinte en mis versos. (p. 202)

Although men, especially employers, were to become close and lasting friends, "las mujeres no querían a Plácido," as Bar-Lewaw observes (p. 35). Handsome, probably charming—at least part of the time—why was the poet so unsuccessful with women? Why was he so disinclined or unable to form permanent attachments with them? His pre-marital affairs were short-lived, with tragic endings, whereupon, on at least one occasion, he contemplated suicide. And his marriage was of especially short duration.

Childhood

Plácido's life may be conveniently divided into six general periods: first, the Havana period, from birth in 1809 until 1826, years in which he received his scant formal education and was apprenticed in various trades; second, his first residence in Matanzas, from 1826 to 1832, when he became proficient as a carver of tortoise-shell combs; third, another residence in the capital, from 1832 to 1836, a period during which, on the occasion of a poetry contest, he achieved his first notoriety; fourth, a second stay in Matanzas, from 1836 to 1840, when he reached the height of his success; fifth, from 1840 until his last and final imprisonment, a period which he spent in towns east of Matanzas and incurred the suspicion of the Spanish government; and sixth, the five months of imprisonment, January 30 to June 28, 1844, when he wrote the sincere and moving poetry by which he attained fame not only in Cuba, Spanish America, and Spain, but in the United States.

Even the facts concerning Plácido's birth are contradictory. Several biographers, for instance, including the French Louis Jourdan, maintained that the poet was born in Matanzas, instead of Havana. Uncertainty surrounded not only the birthplace, but the parents. For some years after Plácido's death, fantastic rumors were spread: according to one, he was the fruit of a clandestine romance between a white woman of high social position and her Negro slave; according to another, he was the offspring of a slave and a member of the Cuban Ministry so distinguished that his name could not be mentioned; then there was the rumor, current in the United States, that Plácido was born a slave.

Some of these errors were corrected upon the discovery of the baptismal certificate in the archives of the Havana orphanage, the Real Casa de Beneficencia y Maternidad.[21] This certificate, No. 1600, states that a baby, *al parecer blanco*, was abandoned there on April 6, 1809, and that, according to a note accompanying the child, the date of birth was March 18. The writer of the certificate, a chaplain by the name of Antonio Eusebio Ramos, added that he immediately baptized the child with the name of Diego Gabriel de la Concepción and that the godfather was Joaquín de Cárdenas, a captain of the militia.

Problems have arisen as a result of this document. For example, why did the chaplain so name the poet? Morales and Calcagno started the story that the note accompanying the baby included not only the date of birth, but a request that this name be used in the certificate, a request that the chaplain saw no need of mentioning. In 1906, however, the "doubting Thomas" Figarola-Caneda, visited the foundling home where he found the certificate, but not the note. Convinced that the two earlier biographers never actually saw such a note and that, if they did, it included no such request, he concluded that the paternal grandmother appeared at the baptism and asked that this name be used.

"Diego" probably came from the father's name, Diego Ferrer Matoso, and "Concepción" from the mother, Concepción Vázquez. Carruthers points out that "Gabriel" may have been chosen because of the "coincidence of the child's birthday with the feast of St. Gabriel which prior to 1921 was celebrated on March 18" (p. 10). One problem easy to answer is the origin of "Valdés,"

---

[21] This document has been widely reproduced: see DOMINGO FIGAROLA-CANEDA, *Plácido (poeta cubano)* (Havana, 1922), p. 240; GARÓFALO MESA, p. 14; HORREGO ESTUCH (1960), pp. 329-330; and others.

not included in the certificate, but added later. Despite Jourdan's careless assumption that this was the name of Plácido's father, rather it was that of the Bishop of Havana, Jerónimo Valdés y Sierra, founder of the orphanage. It was the custom to give his name to all illegitimate children left there.

Not so easy to explain is the reference to the godfather as "Cárdenas," for the respected critic, Bachiller y Morales, insisted that a family friend, the druggest Fernando Plácido Fuentes, played this role, a theory that seems plausible since it would account for the origin of the poet's pen name. With regard to this pseudonym, however, generally accepted is the explanation that at the age of fifteen, the poet took it from the name of the self-effacing hero, whom he very much admired, in a novel by Mme de Genlis (Stéphanie-Félicité du Crest de Saint-Aubin, 1746-1830), a prolific novelist and governess for the children of Philippe Égalité, Duc d'Orléans. The novel was first published in Paris in 1816 as *Les Battuécas* (2 vols.), then appeared in English (New York, 1817), as *Placide, a Spanish Tale,* and, according to Garófalo Mesa (p. 16), it was published as *Plácido y Blanca,* presumably in Spanish.

Another problem raised by the certificate has to do with the chaplain's expression *al parecer blanco*. Several critics jumped to the conclusion that it meant that the baby's color was an indeterminate shade. Others explained that occasionally colored babies tend to be very light-skinned and their adult color cannot be determined for some time. Actually, Plácido, with only one-eighth colored blood, was an *octavón,* to use the word of Horrego Estuch.

Of the famous Cuban charitable institution where Plácido was abandoned, Wurdemann reported that in 1842 it sheltered 604 individuals of both sexes, black and white, sane and insane. It was fairly well-endowed even in Plácido's day; in 1832 it had a capital of $262,505; ten years later it was enjoying an annual income of $86,407. "Well might the Habeneros [sic] be proud of this monument of their charity," wrote Wurdemann, "unexcelled as it is by any similar institution in other countries, in the liberality of its regulation, and the care it bestows on its inmates" (p. 224).

All the earliest biographers, such as Guiteras, Calcagno, the poet's close friend Morales, and Sanguily, flatly maintained, without indicating the source of their information, that Plácido was the illegitimate son of a quadroon father, Diego Ferrer Matoso, a native of Havana and a barber or hairdresser by profession, and a white mother, a dancer from Burgos. Both worked in El Coliseo or the Teatro Principal, Havana's leading theater until it was destroyed by a hurricane in 1846. Guiteras pointed out that this type of miscegenation was unusual in Cuba. Ordinarily such unions took place between white men, often of high social position, and colored women, often of slave status or other inferior class, which made it difficult for them to ward off the advances of their seductors.

Plácido's father is reputed to have been handsome and personable, from a well-to-do family, as free colored families went. As *coiffeur* at the theater, where he no doubt met Concepción, he became friendly with stage celebrities and Havana aristocracy and mixed in an unusually high society. He owned his own carriage, in which Plácido is said to have ridden proudly, and, in the center of Havana, a comparatively elaborate home, with a long patio which led to the dining room and kitchen in the rear. According to Horrego Estuch, he had invested his money in the gamecock business.

Basing their assumption mainly on Plácido's "A Lisio," biographers have believed that Ferrer was addicted to gambling. In this long epistle, Plácido learns that his friend Lisio's consuming vice is gambling. The poet offers sympathy, saying that he, too, has had experience with this evil, although he never personally indulged in it. In the following selection, he confesses that one member of his family, the member who should have been the shining example, was so addicted:

> Yo sin haber jugado un solo día
> También he sido víctima del juego.
> Oye la historia, pues de mi indigencia,
> Y la vista me falte si te miento:
> "En la edad infantil, cuando a mis ojos
> Era este mundo un paraíso inmenso,
> Por ignorar sus faltas rebozadas
> Bajo mentido y deslumbrante velo.
> Era mi casa, no de las más ricas,
> Porque la rectitud de mis abuelos
> Esquivando la pompa, procurara

Un modesto pasar para sus nietos...
Empero mi familia era dichosa,
¡Ay! demasiado con dolor me acuerdo...
Mas el tiempo que todo lo destruye,
Y hasta el mármol y el bronce va deshecho,
A los terribles y continuos golpes
De su hoz potente, y de su planta al peso,
Arrebató la calma de mis lares,
Y en la desgracia nos lanzó sin duelo.
Uno de la familia (a quien me obligan
Dios y la tierra conservar respeto)
El que debiera más que otro ninguno
De una sana moral darnos ejemplo,
De ese vicio fatal se vio vencido...   (pp. 520-521)

It is thought that Ferrer became bankrupt as a result of gambling and of the purchase of the carriage and the *gallería,* luxuries beyond the means of even a well-to-do Negro. In an effort to recoup his fortune, he went to Mexico, but misfortune continued to pursue him. He died there, leaving his mother and son destitute. Presumably any support he had been extending them from Mexico ceased, and Plácido was forced to learn a trade.

It seems likely that Concepción Vázquez abandoned her baby at the orphanage in order to hide her wickedness from society. One critic, lacking facts, compensated with imagination, as seen in the following dramatic explanation: "¿Qué hacer? Darlo a criar a un extraño era vender su propio secreto. ¿Criarlo ella? Imposible. La sociedad civilizada del siglo diez y nueve echaría sobre su rostro la mancha de aquella unión clandestina y de su producto bastardo; la pobre señora no duerme. Aquello le molesta... de pronto, como un relámpago que brilla en medio de una tempestad nocturna, así brilla en la mente de doña Concepción una idea, una luz. ¡La Beneficencia!" [22]

Perhaps Concepción feared that Havana aristocracy would condemn her not so much because of her sexual indiscretion, but because of the racial problem involved. Even then Cuba was fearing a Negro insurrection. As Horrego Estuch points out, just three years later, in 1812, a conspiracy of slaves was discovered and

---

[22] Jesús Saiz de la Mora, *Plácido, su popularidad, su obra, y sus críticos, en el 75º aniversario de su muerte* (Havana, 1919), p. 4.

when the decapitated heads of the captured were exhibited in Havana's central streets, interracial animosity reached a peak. One of Jourdan's few accurate observations may be the following: "Le préjugé de la couleur, toujours souverain en Amérique, mais beaucoup plus absolu à cette époque qu'aujourd'hui, veut que toute union entre personnes de couleurs différentes soit considérée comme une infamie. Aux yeux des blancs, la mère de Plácido était dès lors une femme perdue" (p. vii).

Concepción's cowardice, whether caused by fear of censure for cohabiting out of wedlock or for cohabiting with a Negro, was recognized by her son when, in his famous sonnet "A la fatalidad," he grieved that "entre el materno tálamo y la cuna" she had placed "el férreo muro del honor."

Efforts to whitewash Concepción's treatment of the baby have been based on erroneous facts or questionable reasoning. Since she had nothing to do with raising the child, if for no other reason, Jourdan's observation that "sous une si tendre protection [Concepción's], Plácido épanouit à l'aise ses facultés naissantes et ses premiers sentiments" seems quite misleading (p. viii). A modern critic's defense of her appears even more peculiar: Casals maintains that if she had been a really bad woman, she would have aborted the baby, in order that it not interfere even for a few days with her theatrical career (p. 13).

Concepción's feelings toward her son, when he became an adult, may have changed. Such change of heart is open to conjecture, of course, but as more material comes to light, it would seem that the two were in closer contact than was once supposed. She did not support him publicly; at least there is no record of her visiting him during his imprisonments nor of her attending his execution. But in a letter of September 27, 1843, reproduced by Figarola-Caneda, Plácido mentions that "Sra. Da. Concepción Vázquez" had told him that the lawyer Joaquín de Astray y Caneda (grandfather of Figarola-Caneda) would take on his legal defense during his confinement in the Trinidad prison (pp. 237-239). Thus it might seem that Concepción did help her son in times of crisis, although her efforts were furtive. The fact that in this letter Plácido referred to her not as "mother," but as *señora*, does not necessarily indicate lack of affection; in that day, such formality is said to have occasionally existed between even very close relatives, when one was white, and the other, black.

Sanguily was one of the few to insist that a deep friendship united the two and that Plácido frequently stayed at her home in Havana. Perhaps evidence of this strong tie is to be found in the poet's will. Herein he left her his *eterno reconocimiento;* to be noted also is his reference to a ring which apparently she had given him and which he bequeathed to his wife. Morales maintained that, in a conversation during the time of Plácido's final imprisonment, the latter gave his mother's presence in Cuba as one of the reasons why he had always refused to expatriate himself.

Another partial proof of love may be offered by an unpublished letter, dated February 1, 1901. In answer to a request by the librarian, bibliophile, and scholar in Matanzas, José Augusto Escoto, for details concerning Plácido's life, a certain Manuel Federico D'Aure, also of Matanzas, supplied some recollections. On his father's death in Philadelphia, D'Aure and his widowed mother moved to this Cuban town. There in 1839 Plácido began to frequent their home — this was the period of his second residence in Matanzas. D'Aure's most interesting, if somewhat ungrammatical, recollection concerns the poet's love for Concepción: "Recuerdo que Plácido venía a casa despedirse cuando se iba a la Habana a ver a su madre en los días de su santo y cumpleaño, a la que le llevaba compuesta su poesía, a los pocos días volvía muy contento, lo que satisfacía a mi madre, porque le gustaba ver a un hijo tan amante de su madre. Cuando recibía carta Plácido de su madre también venía a casa a enseñarla a mi mamá. Plácido quería mucho a su madre." [23]

Since no theatrical notices refer to Concepción after 1809, it might be assumed that she left the theater. It is thought that in 1836 she married an impresario named Rosales. Poetry bearing her name has been discovered; appearing in the *Diario de la Habana* (1847, 1848), some of it concerns the death of the aforementioned lawyer. Although without any literary value whatsoever, it

---

[23] Letter included in the Escoto papers, "Plácido Material," Box 17, Bundle III, SAL 475.1.2, Harvard University Library.

might indicate that Plácido naturally came by his facility at improvising. One critic, writing in Madrid five years after Plácido's death, said that at that time Concepción enjoyed a high social position in Havana.[24] It is believed that she lived until at least 1861.

How Plácido left the orphanage and who raised him are questions never conclusively answered. The concensus is that Guiteras was correct in maintaining that Ferrer, at first ignorant of his mistress' abandonment of the baby, later went to the Casa de Beneficencia to acknowledge him as his son and to take him to the house Ferrer shared with his mother and sister—a noble, though misguided act, thought the biographer Piñeyro, for thus the very light-skinned Plácido was known to have colored blood (p. 331). Perhaps, as Morales states, Ferrer's generosity was prompted by the desire to please his mother who was determined to raise her grandchild. Legend has it that she was blind, had once been a slave, but was far more compassionate than Plácido's parents.

As is to be expected, confusion reigns as to Plácido's schooling. From 1819 to 1821 he received some elementary education from a certain Pedro J. de Sol, a native of Havana who was to die in Matanzas in 1858. Apparently Plácido later entered the Colegio de Belén, which accepted colored children, and studied with its founder, Juan Francisco Carballo, from Seville. A family friend, Carballo made it financially possible for Plácido to attend. There, or more likely at El Angel, Plácido studied with the founder of this second school, a man who has come down to posterity with several different names, Francisco Bandarán, Wandarán, Bandiarán, and so forth.[25]

---

[24] EMILIO BRAVO, "Literatura española en Cuba," *Semanario Pintoresco Español*, Madrid, 1849, p. 367.

[25] In a curious handwritten biography of Plácido and another Cuban poet, Francisco Orgaz (1810-73), in the Escoto papers, the following version of Plácido's early schooling is given: "Nació en esta ciudad [Havana] en 1809, y de niño estuvo en la escuela que dirijía la parda Anastasia, en la calle de la Amargura [Pedro J. del Sol's school was located on this street], donde aprendió a leer, pasando luego a la de los Padres Belemitas [presumably the Colegio de Belén] donde ensanchó su conocimiento y más tarde a la que dirijía Barandan en El Angel." This account is unsigned, undated,

It has often been said that Plácido studied French. But Morales, always apologizing for his hero, regretfully admitted that the poet's education was too limited to include any real mastery of foreign languages, "si bien de afición leía y traducía el francés, y esto le permitía el conocer en sus fuentes las bellezas de Racine, de ambos Corneille y de Molière" (p. xxii). Of course Plácido read Peninsular literature; during his adolescence he is supposed to have read whatever Spanish novels and plays were within his reach, developing a special taste for historical novels. Since he worked in newspaper offices and a print shop, possibly some such reading material was available to him.

By today's or almost any other day's standards, Plácido's formal education was indeed scant. And, as Guiteras pointed out, probably his haphazard reading benefited him very little. It would seem safe to assume that his real education came later, when his reading was directed by enlightened friends, such as the "literary dilletante" Manuel González del Valle (1802-84), to whom he dedicated the poem "Las venturas del trabajo"; the druggist, Plácido Fuentes, possibly the poet's godfather; the poet Ramón Vélez Herrera (1808-86); and Ignacio Valdés Machuca (1800-51), to whom, as seen in the following selection, Plácido expressed gratitude for help in learning to understand poetry and apologized for his unpolished style:

A DON IGNACIO VALDÉS MACHUCA

Quien a ti debe nociones
De la dulce poesía
Y más de un favor te debe,
Menos de un verso dedica.
   Él es un cuadro incompleto
De tradiciones antiguas,
En prosa, disimulada
Con el velo de la rima.
   Acójelo tal cual es,
Y no lo hagas en estima

---

and almost illegible. It must have been composed before 1886, however, for the author observes later on that of those concerned with the celebration for Martínez de la Rosa only Vélez Herrera (d. 1886) and Bachiller y Morales (d. 1889) were still living.

> Porque algún mérito tenga,
> Ni por la dicción castiza;
> Puesto que ahora esas dotes
> Ni se atienden, ni se miran,
> Sino por la voluntad
> De éste que te los dedica.   (p. 268)

Plácido's career as an apprentice was more active than his career as a student. Horrego Estuch mentions that the poet was apprenticed to a carpenter; all biographers agree that at about twelve years of age he entered Vicente Escobar's studio in Havana, where he showed unusual talent in drawing and penmanship. Escobar, a Negro dedicated to helping his kinsmen, was a popular, if ungifted, portrait painter in the days before photography and was honored by the Queen Mother in Spain in 1834. About 1823 Plácido became an apprentice typesetter in the shop of José Severino Boloña, a printer, poet, and, in 1840, editor and publisher of the *Diario de la Marina de la Habana*. But at age sixteen Plácido gave up typesetting to learn—under the tutelage of Nicolás Bota y Ponce de León, in the Havana jewelry store of a certain Diego Misa—the more profitable trade of carving tortoise shell. According to Morales, this trade was then a booming one, "a causa de las peinetas y otros adornos de carey que usaba el sexo bello de la Habana" (p. xv).

By this time, probably stimulated by the atmosphere of the print shop and by his friendship with the educated Boloña, Plácido had become known as a poet. (Carruthers points out that during this period the University of Havana, founded in 1728, scarcely deserved the name and that the "real culture of the city was centered in the print shops" [p. 12]. He adds that, considering the extraordinary censorship then prevailing in Cuba, it is surprising how even a printing establishment, much less a university, managed to survive.) At parties held in Boloña's shop and in private homes, poets, including Plácido, amused themselves by improvising verse, especially *décimas*. The new poem would be based on the last line of the previous improvisation.

Plácido is said to have disliked these mental gymnastics, but possessed an inherent knack which soon gained him the reputation of a splendid *repentista*. Morales observed that the young man was a very "fecundo y fácil improvisador: Yo lo vi muchas veces pasarse noches y días enteros en algunos festines, bodas, bautismos, natalicios, de amigos y personas decentes, improvisando *cálamo currente* con temas forzados y difíciles que se la daban a veces por personas doctas con el intento de ponerlo en aprietos o de verlo salir airoso, como siempre surgía por más dificultoso que fuese el tema y trabajoso el consonante. Era prodigiosa su memoria al extremo de conservar íntegros al día siguiente o más las improvisaciones por extensas que fuesen" (pp. xviii-xix).

One of Plácido's cleverest and most satiric improvisations was the following, which, like many of his works, reveals a basic distrust of women. Offered the obviously awkward and uninspiring line, "Regálame un quitrín, dame dinero," he composed the sonnet "Decepción":

> A querer con delirio una enemiga
> Me condujo fatídica mi estrella,
> Y el esquivo desdén que encontré en ella
> Acrisolaba mi mortal fatiga.
> ¡Inhumana! la dije: ¿no te obliga
> La llama de mi amor? Pues eres bella,
> Indícame, por Dios, cuál es aquella
> Senda que quieres que en amarte siga.
> Así la dije, y ella desdeñosa
> Volviendo el rostro en ademán severo
> (Esquivez natural de toda hermosa)
> Me dijo: no te canses majadero
> ¿Quieres verme contigo cariñosa?
> Regálame un quitrín, dame dinero. (p. 12)

Another artful piece of improvisation was that composed when guests at a party tried to trick him into committing sacrilege. Given the compromising line "Besar la cruz es pecado," he extracted himself from the trap quickly and with agility:

> Bostezó Minerva un día
> e hizo una cruz en los labios,
> y sin proferirle agravios
> le dije: "Minerva mía
> yo besar desearía
> esa cruz que te has formado".
> Volvióme el rostro indignado,

Y me respondió ella así:
"¿Usted no sabe que aquí
besar la cruz es pecado?"
(*Horrego Estuch* [1960], pp. 103-104).

Youth

The second period of Plácido's life began in 1826. Then he moved to Matanzas, lying "twenty-two leagues east of the Havana," as Turnbull put it (p. 219). According to Turnbull, the census here in 1827 listed 6333 whites, 1941 free colored, and 3067 slaves. Wurdemann reported the census of 1841 as listing 10,304 whites, 3041 free colored, and 5779 slaves. If these figures are accurate, the population increase during fourteen years was remarkable. Such an increase was indeed possible, for, as the statistician Ramón de la Sagra pointed out, great prosperity came to Matanzas in 1806 when it began to export sugar, coffee, and honey. Soon it became Cuba's second city in commercial importance.

Matanzas produced poets, too. Although Plácido was not born there, some of his contemporary bards were, such as José Jacinto Milanés; others, like Domingo del Monte, resided there. Since it was the home of many distinguished literati, it was often referred to as the "Athens of Cuba," although, paradoxically, its name is "Slaughter." Several legends have arisen as to the origin of this name: perhaps the town was once the site of a slaughterhouse; more likely it witnessed human massacres, either of the Spanish by Indians or French pirates, or, even more likely, of Indians by Spanish; and, of course, in 1844, as the scene of the *Conspiración de la Escalera*, it was to witness the slaughter of Negroes.

Bryant, unlike the majority of tourists who never venture out of Havana, traveled to this town situated on a bay even more magnificent than the capital's. Two rivers flow through Matanzas, one of which, the Yumurí, forms the most beautiful valley in Cuba. After climbing to the heights above the town, Bryant wrote the following glowing description: "There lay the valley of the Yumuri, and a sight of it is worth a voyage to the island. In regard to this, my expectations suffered no disappointment. Before me lay a deep valley, surrounded on all sides by hills and mountains, with the little river Yumuri twining at the bottom... The broad fields below were waving with cane and maize, and cottages of the *monteros* were scattered among them, each with its tuft of bamboos and its little grove of plantains... to the west, in a soft golden haze, rose summit behind summit, and over them all, loftiest and most remote, towered the mountain called the *Pan de Matanzas*" (II, 135-136).

Into such a setting Plácido passed in company with Bota, who had taught him the art of combmaking and who had become, as Boloña had and as Morales would later, an intimate friend as well as employer. Presumably by this time Plácido was so skilled in the carving of the ornate combs that Bota urged him to come along, when the shop was moved from Havana to Matanzas.

Probably Plácido's avocation served as a welcome change from this monotonous vocation. He continued to exercise his talent for improvising verse or, aided by a prodigious memory, for reciting poetry thought out days previously. Invited to parties in Matanzas, he sometimes presented to wealthy and distinguished hosts laudatory poems which, according to Guiteras, the poet had lettered on silk and framed with some sort of gold work.

The avocation may have served not only as a welcome relief, but as a source of additional income. The same critic observed that Plácido was often recompensed with one, two, or even three ounces of gold from individuals desiring occasional verse in honor of sweethearts and sponsors or from newspapers wishing to honor rulers and important people. According to others, however, in return for hundreds of these compositions he received neither money nor thanks. But the applause following his recitations —tremendous applause, so it is said—must have pleased him, and so must the title which he soon acquired, "Vate del Yumurí." Probably he was in his element, even though poor.

Legend has it that Plácido and some friends went into the countryside one afternoon to enjoy a view of the valley. In a scenic spot near a stream or fountain, these friends asked him to improvise a poem against slavery. He complied, offering one of his most famous sonnets, "El juramento," distinguished for its precision and economy of words. It was definitely composed in

Matanzas, but some doubt exists as to whether it was composed there during this first residence or later:

> A la sombra de un árbol empinado
> Que está de un ancho valle a la salida,
> Hay una fuente que a beber convida
> De su líquido puro y argentado.
> Allí fui yo por mi deber llamado
> Y haciendo altar la tierra endurecida,
> Ante el sagrado código de vida,
> Extendidas mis manos, he jurado:
> Ser enemigo eterno del tirano,
> Manchar, si me es posible, mis vestidos,
> Con su execrable sangre, por mi mano.
> Derramarla con golpes repetidos;
> Y morir a las manos de un verdugo
> Si es necesario, por romper el yugo.
> (*Horrego Estuch* [1960], pp. 55-56)

It was once believed that Plácido remained in Matanzas the rest of his life. Now, however, it is known that he made many trips back and forth between this town and Havana and re-established residence in the latter city from 1832 to 1836, where he continued his comb business. During this third period he became the favorite of literary dilletantes, partly the result of his participation in a celebration, held in 1834, in honor of the Peninsular poet and dramatist, Francisco Martínez de la Rosa (1787-1862).

The Spaniard's *Conjuración de Venecia* was performed on the Madrid stage that same year; this, his best-known work, is considered of historical importance because it helped to start in Spain the vogue for romantic drama. Like many romanticists, Martínez de la Rosa was involved not only with liberal movements in literature, but in politics, too. Fernando VII once banished him, but on the former's death in 1833, the Queen Regent, in desperation, appointed the author as her Prime Minister. She hoped he could appease the legitimists outraged that the Salic Law had been disregarded by passing the crown to Fernando's infant daughter Isabel II, rather than to his brother, Don Carlos de Borbón.

Perhaps because, as a liberal, Martínez de la Rosa was viewed sympathetically by Cubans or because they hoped, through him and his high position, to obtain some benefits and reform for the Island, an act of hommage, in the form of a poetry contest, was arranged by Havana's literary leaders. Those most instrumental in bringing it about were the poet Francisco Iturrondo (1800-68), to whom Plácido sometimes referred in verse as "Delio," and two of the friends who helped to guide his education, Valdés Machuca ("Desval") and González del Valle ("Dorilo"). The ceremony took place May 1 at an estate called *Las Delicias,* situated in the suburb of Arroyo Apolo, on the banks of the Almendares River outside Havana.

The story goes that each of the thirteen contestants, including Plácido, the poet Vélez Herrera, and the critic and biographer Bachiller y Morales, were dressed in white, with blue ribbons around their necks. To the right of these young men, in semicircle formation, stood their ladies, fiancées, or relatives; they numbered only twelve, since Plácido had none—he was mourning Rafaela's death. The girls represented the nine muses, Sappho, and two rivers, the Almendares and Madrid's Manzanares. In front of the group was erected the temple of Apollo, with a pyre at its base. A human Apollo awarded the crown of laurel to the winner— Plácido! The winner was to hand it on to his lady; in Rafaela's absence, Plácido returned it to Apollo.

The thirteen laudatory poems were published in a pamphlet, *Aureola poética a Don Francisco Martínez de la Rosa por las musas del Almendares* (Havana, 1834), a copy of which was sent to the Prime Minister. It is said that for "La siempreviva," his prize-winning contribution to this aureole of poetry, Plácido received a personal letter of thanks from Martínez de la Rosa and an invitation to visit the Peninsula. Although friends are believed to have raised two thousand pesos for the trip, Plácido declined with words to the effect that he was too much a Cuban ever to leave his beloved homeland. Some biographers add that he asked to use the money to start a small business, but was told it had been collected solely for the purpose of a trip. "Entonces dispón de él," he is supposed to have retorted. [26]

---

[26] HORREGO ESTUCH (1960), p. 110; see also EMILIO BLANCHET, *El Album,* Matanzas, June 28, 1904, no page numbers, cited by Carruthers, p. 28.

This was the romantic period in literature. Perhaps only during such a period could a poet so dramatically achieve fame overnight. One is reminded of a similar, though far more celebrated, instance in Spain, when another young romanticist, José Zorrilla, recited in 1837 an impassioned poem at the funeral service for the beloved Mariano José de Larra and thereupon attained sudden fame. Plácido's recital, in front of his "betters," must have required the same sense of the dramatic, the same courage and abandon as did Zorrilla's. In the following stanza from "La siempreviva," Plácido described himself as a naked youth armed only with daring, not with talent and education, as he entered the bloody battle and played his golden lyre:

> Cual de bélico ardor arrebatado
> El desnudo mancebo se presenta,
> Sólo de noble atrevimiento armado
> En el estruendo de la lid sangrienta;
> Así yo vuelo impávido, animado
> De gloria al soplo que mi pecho alienta,
> Y pulso entre los vates la áurea lira,
> Aunque ni el arte ni el saber me inspira. (p. 637)

Thus by the year 1834, at twenty-five years of age, Plácido had attained considerable fame; soon he was to become its victim. Flushed with success, he wrote poems of a political nature more daring than ever before, and because of these works and his increasing popularity among his countrymen, he fell under the suspicion of the Spanish government. Some critics think that at this time, the very outspoken *décima*, "¡Habaneros, libertad!," was composed:

> ¿O somos libres o no?
> Pues nos burla el orbe entero,
> Si sois salvaje, no quiero
> Morar con vosotros yo,
> Ya el tiempo feudal pasó
> De opresión y obscuridad,
> Oíd en la inmensidad
> Do el regio planeta habita,
> Que una voz de gloria grita:
> ¡Habaneros, libertad!
>   (*Horrego Estuch* [1960], p. 69).

This boldness is evident also in the ode now referred to as "La sombra de Padilla." Supposedly it was written toward the end of this same year, when as customary a festival was being planned to celebrate the Queen's birthday, November 18. Most daring was the following stanza, for which Plácido may have been jailed briefly, to be released through the intervention of a friend, Havana's mayor, Francisco Chacón Calvo:

> Sabia y excelsa Reina, a quien admira
> Extasiado de gozo el pueblo hispano,
> Oye la voz de un vate que respira
> Aura de Libertad, oye un Cubano.
> Alguno habrá que con dorada lira
> Más digna de tu oído soberano,
> Cuando sus cuerdas diamantinas vibre,
> Cante más grato; pero no más libre.   (p. 646)

Perhaps this sudden success sounded hollow in the poet's ear, for although he had won the admiration of cultured literati, he could not change the fact that he was a mulatto. Piñeyro observed that "entonces en Cuba el más rudo e ignorante campesino, venido del fondo de Galicia o de León, se juzgaba un ser superior a todos los mulatos, y al poco tiempo de estar allí creía tener el derecho de que todo hombre de color, por libre que fuera, le hablase con respeto de inferior, con el sombrero en la mano" (pp. 343-344).

The fourth period in Plácido's short life, when he received his greatest honors, began in 1836, the year he left Havana to return to live in Matanzas, and lasted until 1840. Perhaps this departure from the capital was prompted by disgust at his mother's affair with the impresario Rosales, whom she was later to marry. More likely, the return was prompted by an offer of work from another close friend, Dámaso García, who owned a shop where tortoise-shell articles were sold. Plácido did more than carve combs, however; a few months after his arrival, he began to supply the local daily, *La Aurora de Matanzas*, with a poem per issue. As the *Aurora's* official poet, his salary was twenty-five pesos a month until 1842, when, according to Morales, the paper's editor, it was raised to thirty.

At this time a deep friendship between Morales, the editor-botanist, and Plácido, the poet-combmaker, began. Morales wrote, with evident pride, that, in preparation for his book on Cuban flora, the two took long walks together along the banks of the Yumurí where they studied nature. On one of these walks Plácido recited "El juramento," which he may have composed during his previous residence in Matanzas. But occasionally he would suddenly, without any explanation, leave his friend and Matanzas to board a coastal steamer plying between there and Havana, where he would stay for weeks at a time. Apparently he was subject to strange moods and wanderlust. If the supposition is correct, however, that he was fonder of his mother than was once believed, one might suspect that these secret trips were made to see her.

An honor, second only to the winning of the contest of 1834, now came Plácido's way, according to evidence offered by Guiteras, Morales, and a poem. The honor consisted of a visit from one of Cuba's most celebrated poets, the exiled José María Heredia. Allowed to return to his native land for the briefest of visits, he hurriedly passed through Matanzas where he stopped to introduce himself to Plácido.[27] To thank the aristocratic and more famous bard, the grateful mulatto composed "El eco de la gruta." It must have contained serious political implications, for the copy given to Heredia was sealed, to be opened only when the latter was on the high seas en route back to Mexico; on Plácido's own copy, all but the dedicatory part was erased. Left to posterity, thus, are merely this part and possibly Heredia's complete copy, which has never been found.

There are two versions of the dramatic scene which took place in Matanzas between the great Heredia and the humble Plácido. Figarola-Caneda much preferred Guiteras' straightforward description to the more elaborate and contrived one by Morales.[28]

---

[27] A footnote in *Poesías completas de Plácido* (Paris: Librería Española de Mme C. Denné Schmitz e hijo, 1862), p. 213, explains that "El eco de la gruta" was dedicated to Heredia on his visit to Matanzas in 1834. The visit took place in 1836; Heredia landed in Cuba November 5 of that year and returned to Mexico the beginning of the following.

[28] Morales reproduced the dialogue in *El Pensamiento*, Matanzas, 1880, cited by Figarola-Caneda, pp. 165-167.

Guiteras made less effort to quote word for word, as if a stenographer had been present:

> En uno de sus días de amargura se presentó en la tienda un desconocido, manifestando deseos de verlo. El mozo le dio el recado, y Valdés, creyendo fuese alguno de los muchos majaderos que solían ir a encargarle versos, salió tal como estaba, bien ajeno de esperar encontrarse delante de sí a un individuo de un rostro lleno de expresión inteligente, que alargándole la mano, le dijo gozoso: "Vengo a tener el gusto de ver y conocer a Vd. antes de mi partida para Méjico. Yo soy José María Heredia." Ambos vates estuvieron contemplándose en mudo silencio, hasta que repuesto Valdés de su sorpresa, invitó a Heredia a entrar en la sucia trastienda, excusándose de que lo recibiese en traje tan impropio; porque "bajo nuestro cielo en el calor del medio día", le dijo, "no se puede sufrir la camisa durante las horas de trabajo, y yo me he acostumbrado a trabajar sin ella" (January 1, p. 6).

It is said that Heredia, touched by evidences of Plácido's poverty and misery and because of his own plight sympathetic to those critical of the Cuban government, offered the mulatto money to move to Mexico—a second opportunity, coming only two years after the invitation from Martínez de la Rosa in Spain, for the poet to escape the horrible fate reserved for him in his native land. But again Plácido refused, murmuring a second time that he was too much a Cuban ever to leave. Later, on Heredia's death in 1839, Plácido once more referred to him in verse, in the melancholy elegy, "La malva azul," which ends:

> Mas ¡ay! que solamente
> Brindar puedo a su historia
> Una flor melancólica, inocente,
> Versos a su memoria,
> Llanto a su muerte, y a sus cantos gloria.   (p. 563)

Plácido's most impressive achievement during this period was the publication of a book, probably his first; the other similar project had been abandoned, possibly because the poet disapproved of the portrait to accompany the publication. The collection, generally accepted as the princeps, contains ninety-one poems, counting the nine epigrams as one. It was published by Juan José Romero in Matanzas, with the date 1838. That year the *Aurora,* in a November issue, announced the book's forthcoming appearance, but critics think it did not actually see the light of day until 1839. Plácido is said to have received modest royalties. (Several biographers have insisted on the existence of an earlier collection, published by a certain Pedro Feliú Parelló Carrió from Palma de Mallorca. Passing through Havana, he was impressed by the fame that Plácido had attained as a result of the poetry contest and decided to publish a small collection, no copy of which has been reported extant.)

Later Plácido was to enjoy seeing other of his works printed in book form. In 1840 a drama in verse, *El gran maestre de Santiago Vasco López,* was to be published, but for a now unknown reason the publication was canceled. In 1841, however, *El Veguero* appeared, containing "El eco de la gruta," as well as the poem which gives the collection its title. The following year another *Veguero* was printed, possibly simply a second edition, possibly a somewhat different collection. Again certain critics point to a collection whose existence others, such as Eligio de la Puente, deny—an 1842 edition supposedly published by José Sotomayor, whom Plácido mentioned in his will as having purchased verse. De la Puente believes this Sotomayor collection was simply *El veguero,* the first or second version, or perhaps the poetic legend *El hijo de maldición,* which appeared in Matanzas in 1843. At least one collection bearing the date 1842 was printed, however, for a copy is preserved among the papers of the traveler Wurdemann; according to Guiteras and De la Puente, this edition was not actually published until 1846. Thus, Plácido lived to see at least three different books of his own in print. The other editions, today almost as rare and difficult to obtain as the early ones, are all posthumous.[29]

---

[29] For detailed accounts of the editions of Plácido's poetry, see Pedro José Guiteras, "Estudios de la literatura cubana, Gabriel de la Concepción Valdés," *El Mundo Nuevo,* New York, 1874, February 1, p. 43; Francisco Calcagno, *Diccionario biográfico cubano* (New York, 1878), pp. 511-512, and *Poetas de color,* p. 19; Francisco P. de Coronado, "Centenario de Plácido," *La Discusión,* Havana, March 20, 1909, pp. 9, 12; and *Poesías selectas de Plácido,* ed. Eligio de la Puente (Havana, 1930), pp. xix-xxxiii.

All was not honor and success during the period in Matanzas, from 1836 to 1840, however. Plácido had become a victim of his fame not only because he aroused the suspicion of the Spanish government, but because he was besieged for occasional verse, to the point that, by force, his poetizing became almost mechanical. The composition for money of such verse, for birthdays, condolences, and so forth, and the recitations at *tertulias* became drudgery. Expressing disgust with this trafficking in art, Plácido, in the last lines of "A Elino, un consejo," devised a scheme for ridding himself of this onerous task—by demanding prepayment:

> Siguiendo tal norma, Elino,
> Haz quince o veinte sonetos,
> Y cuando te pidan uno
> Donde diga Antón, pon Diego.
> Post data. Pide prestado
> Antes de darlo, y con eso
> Verás cómo todos huyen
> De mandarte hacer sonetos.   (p. 172)

And in a somewhat vicious sonnet, "A mi cumpleaños," Plácido yearned for a perfect birthday when the bargain hunters in verse would be cruelly punished:

> No quiero que de púrpura y de nieve
> Vista el oriente en mi natal la aurora,
> Ni que Erato en su cítara sonora
> Mi nombre al Pindo generosa lleve,
> Ni que el Eterno mi canción eleve
> Al sacro Empíreo donde reina y mora,
> Ni que me brinde mi adorada Flora
> Que el dulce beso de sus labios pruebe;
> Ni que mueva mi voz los troncos rudos,
> Ni que alaben mis obras los discretos,
> Ni en la guerra ganar bandas y escudos.
> Todos mis gozos quedarán completos,
> Con que se vuelvan ciegos, mancos, mudos,
> Cuantos piensen mandarme hacer sonetos.   (p. 7)

The shame Plácido felt at prostituting his talent was probably heightened by the appearance of "El poeta envilecido," first published in *El Plantel* (Havana, 1838). Its author, the rising young white poet, José Jacinto Milanés (1814-63), roundly reproached an unnamed writer, undoubtedly Plácido, for degrading himself at the feet of the wealthy:

> Por más que su alma presuma
> Hácele tomar la pluma
> Necesidad.
> Y en su mal nacida rima
> La adulación se echa encima
> De la verdad.
> Torpe ... que a su pensamiento
> Siendo libre como el viento
> Por alto don,
> Le corta el ala, le oculta,
> Y en la cárcel le sepulta
> Del corazón.
> Y ¿qué es mirar a ese vate
> Ser escabel del magnate,
> Cuando el festín,
> Cantar sin rubor ni seso,
> Y disputar algún hueso
> Con el mastín?
> (*Horrego Estuch* [1960], pp. 89-90)

If the additional stanzas appearing in a later edition of Milanés' complete works (New York, 1865) are genuine—a government censor might have suppressed them in the 1838 publication in Havana—the white poet was attacking also the color of Plácido's skin. According to Figarola-Caneda and Milanés' friend, the literary dilletante Domingo del Monte, *cobrizo* is an allusion to Plácido, and *negro* an allusion to another Cuban poet, Juan Francisco Manzano:

> Y si la suerte le hizo
> De color negro o cobrizo,
> ¡Mísero de él!
> Pues su horizonte es sombrío,
> Su aire seco, su sol frío,
> Su amor de hiel.
> (*Figarola-Caneda*, p. 201)

Figarola-Caneda—who devoted a substantial portion of his biography to correspondence, including some with Milanés' brother, concerning the white poet's malice—concluded that the latter was attacking simply the circumstances which vilify an author, not the author himself. Others have indignantly denounced Milanés; they believe that he was exceedingly ungallant, if nothing else, especially in view of the fact that just before the appearance of his poem, Plácido had published a sonnet, "A José Jacinto Milanés," in high praise of Milanés' chivalric drama, *El Conde Alarcos* (1838). Throughout their lives, the two poets found themselves in competition. For instance, the similarity of Plácido's "A un pajarillo" to Milanés' "La fuga de la tórtola" aroused suspicion; the basic idea of humanity's desire for freedom is expressed in somewhat the same way in both works.

Possibly about this time, 1838, Plácido was arrested again; again, that is, if he actually were arrested before because of his outspoken political poetry. Probably the arrest occurred in Havana, on one of the poet's frequent trips there, and he was imprisoned for seven days. This time his crime was a trivial debt. Evident it is that budgeting was not one of his long suits; if he came into money, he spent, lent, or gave it away; probably in the same casual manner, he borrowed it. Proof that he was not averse to borrowing may be offered by a copy, signed by a Juan Guiteras, of Plácido's promissory note, dated December 14, 1842: "Debo a el Sor. Ledo. D. Juan Nepumuceno Valiente, la cantidad de siete pesos, q. serán pagados en el término de veinte y cuatro horas." [30]

In 1839 a final honor was bestowed on Plácido, in the form of a visit from another celebrity, almost as distinguished as Heredia, and, like Heredia, exiled to Mexico from his native Cuba because of separatist leanings. This visitor, Andrés de la Flor, who had become a general in the Mexican army, discussed with Plácido the sad plight of their homeland. As he did with Heredia, Plácido presented his honored guest with a poem, in this case entitled "Al general mexicano," sealed and not to be opened until the recipient had left Cuban shores. It is well the work was not circulated in Cuba, for it is extremely outspoken, as evidenced by the following selection:

> Es verdad que el camino de la gloria
> Tu espada y tu valor te lo han abierto,

---

[30] This note forms part of the Escoto papers.

Marcándote una página en la historia;
Mas también por desdicha es harto cierto
Que hay en tu patria hermosa y desgraciada
Millares de hombres fuertes e instruidos
En la inacción y esclavitud sumidos,
Que con valor y espada,
Héroes pudieron ser, y no son nada.
(Horrego Estuch [1960], p. 108)

Villa Clara

The fifth period, from 1840 to Plácido's final imprisonment, witnessed a series of trips from Matanzas eastward, especially to Villa Clara. (Cuban geographic nomenclature may be very confusing to a foreigner; particularly confusing is the fact that the name of the capital, Villa Clara, has been changed to Santa Clara, and the name of its province, lying just east of that of Matanzas, has been changed from Santa Clara to Las Villas, this last term used also to refer to five towns—Santa Clara, Trinidad, Remedios, Cienfuegos, and Sancti Spiritus.) Presumably Plácido made these journeys in search of additional income. Vagueness exists as to their frequency and length of duration, possibly because friends, fearing to be identified as such during the purges and executions, destroyed documents relating to him. There is proof of at least two trips to Villa Clara, however, and on the first, undertaken in February, 1840, he may have stayed as long as ten months.

This first trip was supposedly made on three ounces of gold which Morales, as editor of the *Aurora* in Matanzas, advanced him. The story goes that ten days later Plácido handed his friend, astonished at the poet's ability to compose so much in so short a time, a rolled-up manuscript which paid up the loan. It contained poems, some of which are now considered to rank with his very best: "A Polonia," "A Grecia," "A Venecia," "Una lágrima de sangre," and a long composition of which part had already been published with the title of "El pirata." The first work was exceptionally daring, for "Cuba" could easily be substituted for "Poland":

Calma, nación heroica, tu agonía,
Y contempla olvidando tus horrores,

Que mil pueblos se hicieron opresores
Y sufrieron después la tiranía.
　　Medio siglo cabal no ha todavía
Que en Moscou y Marengo tus señores
Delante de los galos vencedores
Abatieron sus águilas un día.
　　Si andando el tiempo con la Europa embiste
Horda inmensa de bárbaros armada
Y ves al Zar doblar la frente triste,
　　Exclamarás a su enemiga aliada:
"Esas son las cadenas que me diste,
Tuyas son, te las vuelvo, estoy vengada."　　(p. 34)

Upon leaving Matanzas for Villa Clara, it would seem as if Plácido felt that he was saying goodby to one period of his life, a period spent in homes that were anything but elegant. One of them is satirically described in the clever "Mi casa," the first stanzas of which are:

　　　Quiero a los que me procuren
(Que hartos son por mi desgracia)
Para evitarles molestias,
Dar las señas de mi casa.
　　No indico calle ninguna;
Pues cual marabú que vaga
Errante por el desierto
Con su tienda de campaña,
　　Suelo mudarme a ocasiones
Tres veces a la semana;
Y así tengo por más cuerdo
Bosquejarles mi morada.
　　Supuesto que ella es la misma
Doquier que Plácido vaya,
Pintando la que ahora vivo,
Están las demás pintadas.
　　Cuando veáis una puerta
Que jamás esté cerrada
(Porque donde nada existe
¿Para qué llaves ni aldabas?)
　　Dirigid la vista al centro,
Encontraréis una cama,
Tres sillas, que fueron nuevas
En tiempo de doña Urraca,
　　Una mesa tan ruinosa
Que sólo tiene tres patas;

En un cordel, que es la percha,
Veréis dos piezas colgadas;
  ¡Es mi ropa de más lujo
Para los Corpus y Pascuas!
Son dos camisas ¡oh amigos!
Guardaos bien de tocarlas.   (p. 133)

Carruthers believes this year of 1840 in Villa Clara was "perhaps the happiest" of the poet's life (p. 50). Plácido certainly did praise highly both the town and the friends made there, in poems like "El veguero," the work featured in the collection of 1841 by the same name. An important cause of his happiness may have been the opportunity to contribute to the local tri-weekly, *El Eco de Villa-Clara,* the second oldest newspaper of central Cuba. Through the publisher, Manuel de Sed, Plácido is said to have met many intellectuals, both black and white, some of whom invited him to their homes. He also plied his trade of combmaking, first in the shop of a certain Juan Bautista Moya and later perhaps in an atelier in the palatial home of the wealthy Manuel Jiménez Peña.

Possibly another reason for Plácido's love of Villa Clara was the town's chief diversion, cockfighting, apparently the only one of his father's vices which he had inherited. As a joke, Moya sent the poet six mortally wounded gamecocks to restore to health. He responded with the following amusing epigram:

Moya, los hados fatales
Por una incidencia rara,
Me hacen ser en Villa Clara
Enfermero de animales.
Pero ya que tú te vales
De sátiras contra mí,
Manda animales, que aquí,
Los curaré sin demora,
Hasta que llegue la hora
De hacerte un remedio a ti.   (p. 494)

Plácido's most famous poem dealing with this so-called sport is the fable "Los dos gallos." Amazingly applicable to his own life is the moral he drew that everything depends on blind fortune, that today's hero is tomorrow's villain:

> Brinca-cercas, un gallo valeroso,
> Vencedor de las riñas más tremendas,
> Hallóse cierta vez con Trabucazo,
> Que también valentón nombrado era.
>   A los primeros tiros cayó herido
> Con una pata menos Brinca-cercas;
> Mandólo el amo levantar al punto,
> Y ganó Trabucazo la pelea.
>   Cantó con arrogancia, escarbó el suelo,
> Haciendo del contrario larga befa.
> Un mes tras otro fuéronse hasta un año,
> Volviéronse a encontrar por contingencia,
>   Y el primero le dijo: —Ola Trabuco,
> Mira hoy donde guardas la cabeza,
> Porque sólo que tu amo te la quite,
> La podrás libertar de mis espuelas.
>   —Menos palabras—contestó Trabuco,
> —Pues si vivo escapaste en la otra fiesta,
> Como te pique firme por la barba,
> No te daré lugar a brincar cercas.
>   Abosáronse al fin los dos contrarios,
> Y Trabuco empezó con tal braveza,
> Que ya contó cumplir con su palabra
> Y dijo para sí: —la cosa es hecha.
>   El bravo Brinca-cercas le seguía
> Como el que está velando a quien le vela,
> Y cuando menos lo esperó Trabuco
> Cayó de un tiro desnucado en tierra.
>   Entonces en silencio se quedaron
> Los que aplaudieron su primer pelea,
> Y los que le llamaron invencible,
> Hoy con placer al vencedor celebran.
>   ¡Así pasan las cosas de este mundo!
> Pendientes todas de fortuna ciega,
> Al que hoy es victorioso y aplaudido,
> Si es vencido mañana, lo desprecian.   (pp. 335-336)

Certainly there was much to prevent Plácido's enjoyment of life in Villa Clara. First, he must have been disturbed by the large proportion of slaves there — 886, according to Wurdemann's figures of 1844, with 1891 free colored and 3855 whites. Secondly, he was probably apprehensive of the turn of political events; in 1840 several important citizens of Villa Clara took part in an abortive expedition of revolt against Spain. Thirdly, the poet must have been frustrated by the rigid censorship being exerted, even on fiction, as was the author of the following protest published in the *Eco* (March 19, 1843): "Mas, ¿por qué se priva en Cuba a los literatos de la libertad de escribir? ¿Qué se teme de una comedia, de un tomo de poesías, de una novela de costumbres, de un periódico literario? ¿Alguna insurrección por ventura?, ¿qué, pues, de dos censores para las obras puramente de imaginación, lo mismo que para las observaciones políticas? ¡Eso es monstruoso, es inconcebible, y sólo ha podido producirlo el delirio de algunos espantadizos, que por todas partes sólo ven fantasmas!" [31]

The suspicion Plácido had already aroused among Spanish authorities by sedition-tinged poetry was probably increased now by his frequent, unexplained trips around and about Villa Clara. He was undoubtedly well aware of this suspicion; he could not have failed to be, if the contention of certain critics is well-founded — they contend that in 1840 the poet was imprisoned for one night on no specific charge, by order of the governor of that area, Lieutenant Colonel Aniceto Valverde, and then released upon the intervention of a rich planter and patron of the arts, Antonio Mesa Santamaría. Possibly a proof of Plácido's awareness of the danger he was running are the lines that he composed the same year when, in the cementery of Villa Clara, he and a friend noticed a beautiful flower growing out of a skull:

> Bella flor, ¿por qué naciste?
> ¡Qué funesta fue tu muerte!
> Saliste a buscar la vida
> Y te hallaste con la muerte.   (*Garófalo Mesa*, p. 47)

Plácido did indeed love the countryside. As he had done in Matanzas, so in Villa Clara he took long walks to enjoy nature. On one such occasion he christened a nearby stream with the name *Bélico;* his curious explanation for this name is given in a note to his poem of farewell "A mis amigos de Villa-Clara." [32] On

---

[31] Cited by Garófalo Mesa, p. 36.
[32] "El arroyo que circunda esta Villa, que hoy puede llamarse almacén general del comercio terrestre, aún no tiene nombre, y me creo tan autorizado como cualquiera para darle éste, atendiendo a que en su orilla es un mineral de imán, y en su margen nacen laureles, símbolos el primero de la guerra, y los segundos de la victoria" (Garófalo Mesa, p. 46).

another occasion he came upon a river which reminded him of the Yumurí, at whose banks he had composed "El juramento," during one of his stays in Matanzas. Here to friends he recited the poem from memory; this additional recitation probably accounts for the fact that certain critics once maintained he composed the work in Villa Clara.

At the end of 1840 Plácido returned to Matanzas where he continued writing for both the *Aurora* and the *Eco*. During this last residence in Matanzas, several strange events took place, and his marriage might be considered one of the strangest. Horrego Estuch tells of another: on one of the poet's many trips to the capital, a slave named Dolores was hit by a cart; more disturbed by the damage to her finery than by that to her body, Dolores reported to authorities that the guilty driver was colored. It took Plácido a week in jail to prove his innocence.

Under unusual circumstances two mediocre poems were written during this period. In May, 1841, Plácido composed a work in honor of Manuel Francisco García, a parish priest in Matanzas whom Plácido had known for many years. The occasion for so honoring this good friend was the laying of a cornerstone for a nave being constructed in his parochial church. In September of the following year, on another of the poet's furtive visits to Havana, he witnessed the landing of the steamer "Natche," which had miraculously survived a terrible storm. As the exhausted passengers disembarked, the spectators asked Plácido to compose a poem on the spot, a request which he granted with a sonnet.

Because the data is scant and conflicting, it is impossible to determine accurately Plácido's comings and goings and arrests, from the time of his marriage November 27, 1842, to his final imprisonment in Matanzas. But in the letter to the lawyer Astray, Plácido mentioned that on March 2, 1843 he left Matanzas to return to his beloved province of Santa Clara. (At this time he thus abandoned his bride of only three months.) Reaching Sagua la Grande by boat in two days, he then proceeded to the province's capital, arriving there the afternoon of the next day.

The most recent account of the first serious plot in which Plácido was involved, the beginning of the end, so to speak, is that of Horrego Estuch. According to him, a certain ambitious woman,

Leonor Morejón, owned a farm on the coast where slaves from Africa were secretly landed and sold by her lover, the bandit José Joaquín Clavel. One night the latter stabbed to death the planter Francisco Arencibia and two onlookers, passers-by. The motive for the murder was twofold, theft and revenge — Clavel was attempting to rob Arencibia's plantation, and once this planter had flogged Leonor. Desiring to escape the garrote, the two lovers conceived the idea of reporting to the Governor of Santa Clara, Valverde, the tale that the three murdered men, one of them English, had asked Clavel to help in inciting a Negro insurrection. Later, in an anonymous accusation sent to the authorities on April 1, 1843, Plácido was numbered among the inciters. [33]

As a result of this accusation, Plácido, upon returning to Villa Clara on April 5 or 6, 1843, from a trip to Cienfuegos, was arrested along with a white friend, Santiago Beltrán, and Leonor's sinister brother, Ramón "el León." Probably the three were sent to the prison, called La Ferrolana, in Trinidad, Cuba's third oldest town. On April 18 legal proceedings are said to have been begun against them in Villa Clara. Probably Plácido remained in prison for six months, from April to October 11, when the order for his release was given.

Undoubtedly the release was secured by Astray, to whom, as aforementioned, Plácido wrote from the Trinidad prison on September 27, 1843, saying that, according to his mother, Astray would take on his defense. It is thought that the lawyer's intervention was reluctant — understandably, considering the very serious charges involved.

Considerable proof that Plácido was imprisoned in Trinidad for six months is thus offered by this letter (if it is genuine), as reproduced by Figarola-Caneda (pp. 237-239). In it Plácido wrote that he was arrested in his home in Villa Clara at midnight, after returning from Cienfuegos. He protested that, although his belongings were searched and nothing incriminating found, he had been under duress (just what kind, he does not specify — presumably incarceration). He added that by October 6 he would have been so persecuted for six months.

---

[33] See the anonymous letter as reproduced by Horrego Estuch (1960), pp. 333-337.

Further proof of the long imprisonment is given by a document reproduced by Horrego Estuch ([1960], pp. 338-339). This is the report of November 15, 1843, from the Governor of Trinidad, Pedro de la Peña, warning the Governor of Matanzas, where Plácido was to go two days later, that the poet had been in jail in Trinidad for six months, that since his release, his behavior had not been good, he had found no work, and he should be kept under constant surveillance.

Other versions, much less credible, of the poet's whereabouts during this period have been given. Carruthers maintained that Plácido was indeed arrested April 6 in Villa Clara, but was sent to prison in Havana, rather than in Trinidad, and kept there until August 30.[34] Thereupon he returned to Matanzas where he shut himself up for almost a week to produce some fifty-five compositions for the *Aurora*, with which to finance a trip to Trinidad. There he finally arrived, in the company of two friends whose names are now forgotten. After a very short stay, he was imprisoned locally by order of Brigadier Pedro de la Peña. According to this version, his imprisonment thus lasted only about two months.

The early biographers do not refer to the arrest in Villa Clara in April or to the imprisonment at this time in either Havana or Trinidad. They relate that freely and on his own Plácido went to Trinidad where he was arrested much later. Of course by now he had to account to the authorities for his trips; for this one, the biographers maintain that he gave the excuse of wanting to witness the religious activities of Holy Week. It is undeniable that some religious influence swayed him at this time, for in Trinidad he produced several of his best religious poems, such as "A la muerte de Jesucristo" and "A la resurrección." Perhaps they were composed in prison, out of sight of the processions.

On the "Cisne," sailing from the port of Casilda, November 17, 1843, almost a year after his marriage, Plácido left Trinidad for Matanzas. The steamer stopped for two days in Cienfuegos, where Plácido visited with old friends. Guiteras reported that Plácido

---

[34] See documents reproduced by Roberto P. De Acevedo and Benito Alonso y Artigas, "Nuevas noticias y documentos del poeta Plácido," *El País*, Havana, February 25, 1941, p. 12, cited by Carruthers, pp. 68-71.

arrived in Matanzas in remarkably good humor, despite the *affaire Trinidad* and despite the fact that he was immediately put under partial surveillance, a result no doubt of Peña's warning to the Governor of Matanzas. (This surveillance may soon have become more stringent, upon the outbreak of a Negro insurrection on a nearby plantation.) Questioned by friends in Matanzas as to the mysterious happenings in Trinidad, Plácido explained only that he had been arrested on suspicion of being involved with abolitionists plotting to overthrow slaveholders; since he was innocent and there was no proof of guilt, he was allowed to leave.

Conspiracy and Death

Back in Matanzas before the end of November, Plácido was to find his days of freedom limited in number. On January 30 of the following year, 1844, according to the more recent authorities (on February 29, according to the earlier ones, including Morales), the poet was imprisoned for the last time, first in an old fortress, La Vigía. A few days later he was transferred to the city prison where he remained until twenty-four hours before his execution. On June 12 he and ten fellow prisoners were condemned to death for high treason. On June 22 Captain General Leopoldo O'Donnell approved the sentence, and Plácido was ordered to be taken to the death house in the military hospital of Santa Isabel at six o'clock the morning of June 27. There he would remain, *en capilla*, until the same hour the following day, when he would be led before the firing squad. [35]

In 1843 O'Donnell, observing that he had come to Cuba "no a hacer la felicidad del país, sino a obedecer a España," had taken over the reins of government. [36] Apparently he obeyed well. Exportation of coffee, sugar, and tobacco was greater than ever before. From the economic standpoint his government was

---

[35] See Horrego Estuch (1960), pp. 340-357, for reproductions of the "Sentencia del Tribunal Militar," "Orden de Ejecución de la Sentencia," "Ejecución de la Sentencia," and "Inscripción de Defunción."

[36] José Ignacio Rodríguez, *Vida de don José de la Luz y Caballero* (New York, 1879), p. 143, quoted by Figarola-Caneda, p. 189.

extremely successful, but from the humanitarian one, it was wretched. The new wealth was the direct result of slavery; the number of slaves had risen proportionately to reach its highest figure during his rule.

The General outdid even Tacón, as far as severity and cruelty were concerned — cruelty that was to reach a climax in the *Conspiración de la Escalera*. Guiteras described O'Donnell as "de un carácter vehemente, muy pagado de su capacidad, avaro de riquezas y nada escrupuloso en infringir las leyes" (January 15, p. 23). It is said that the General exacted from his friends, the slave traders, one ounce of gold for each African smuggled into Cuba; this was the protection money the traffickers paid to escape being sentenced for piracy.

O'Donnell played two sides, Spain's and his own, and at the same time avoided open war with England who was demanding that the Spanish cease dealing in slaves and adhere to the treaty of 1817, signed by Fernando VII, a treaty in which it was agreed to sentence slavers for piracy. Although the English were firmly entrenched in Jamaica, center of the business, they were planning to complete manumission in their colonies. Fearful that in world markets the price of their sugar and rum would then exceed Spain's, they insisted slavery be abolished in the Spanish colonies, too. Of course they opposed annexation of Cuba by the United States, for slavery would continue on the Island — the States were still a slave-holding country. (Some historians maintain, however, that England had concluded that in the long run free labor was cheaper than slave, at least as far as the sugar and rum business was concerned.)

To ferret out violations of these abolitionist agreements between Madrid and London, David Turnbull became Consul in Havana, a position which he occupied from November 4, 1840 until June 8, 1842; November 6 of the latter year, upon returning to Cuba from a visit to Nassau, he was forcibly put on the "Thomas," sailing for England. He carried out his duties so scrupulously and efficiently that he incurred the hatred of powerful, corrupt whites. As one Cuban historian observed, "Turnbull era un hombre de hierro, activo y vigilante como pocos; sabía cuanto pasaba en Cuba, y al menor barrunto de expedición, a la más ligera infracción del pacto internacional, acudía con sus reclamaciones perentorias a poner coto al desmán." [37]

Concerning Turnbull's meticulous enforcement of Spain's half-hearted promise not to admit any more slaves into the Island, the following amusing story is told by Wurdemann, in *Notes on Cuba:*

> It is related of the British ex-Consul, Mr. Turnbull, that having discovered a thousand of the negroes exposed in the Havana mart to have been just imported, he hastened to the Captain-General with the news, affirming that he knew also the owners and the vessels that had brought them. The latter, with feigned surprise that the laws should be thus openly broken in the very capital, ordered a company of horse to attend Mr. Turnbull to the spot, and capture both the slaves and the sellers. On the way thither the commanding officer became suddenly indisposed, and getting rapidly worse, was compelled to stop at his house, where several physicians were soon in attendance on him, and his case was pronounced to be very dangerous. In about three hours, however, he was sufficiently relieved to accompany the consul in a volante at the head of his troop, but when they reached the mart, only a few *ladinos* were found there. The next day a bill of two thousand doubloons was sent to the owners of the slaves; one-half as hush-money for the Captain-General, and the other half a remuneration for the physicking the officer of the troop had undergone in their behalf, during which a timely notice had caused them to remove all the *bozales* from the mart. This anecdote, for the truth of which I do not vouch, was circulated in 1841, and is related to show the feelings of the people on the subject (pp. 254-255).

The idea of Negro emancipation had been spreading; as early as 1812—not to speak of those in the eighteenth century—a sizable Negro revolt was crushed. Naturally the British, including Turnbull when he was Consul, were suspected of backing the revolts, perhaps with Plácido's aid. According to an authority on the

---

[37] ENRIQUE JOSÉ VARONA, "El caso de Mr. Turnbull," in José Antonio Saco, *Historia de la esclavitud de la raza africana en el nuevo mundo* (Havana, 1938), IV, 192. Varona's account was first published in *La Semana*, Havana, March 5, 1888.

Conspiración, a more serious incident took place in Matanzas in December, 1843, when a large number of slaves on a nearby plantation plotted a rebellion. The story goes that the slave and mistress of Esteban Santa Cruz de Oviedo, owner of the plantation Trinidad, betrayed the plot in return for her liberty and five hundred pesos. The Governor of Matanzas then commissioned Santa Cruz and the Lieutenant Colonel of the militia, Francisco Hernández de Morejón, to investigate the matter—the former appointment was illegal, of course, for the planter held no official position.[38] This real or imagined plan to rebel was the final indignity, O'Donnell seemed to think; he decided the Negroes should be taught a lesson and demanded absolute power from Spain.

An Inquisition-like "Military Commission" was formed, with Brigadier Fulgencio Salas as President, and, by decree of May 6, 1844, its powers were passed to Matanzas where its flagrant disregard of justice and humaneness became famous. Salas maintained that, when the nation's security was at stake and when crimes against the State were involved, any means whatsoever were justified to settle the matter for the good of the majority. Thereupon, if not before, panic reigned in the colored population, especially in that of Matanzas.

The Commission sent agents to all parts of Cuba to search for and seize suspected recalcitrants—slaves, free colored, mulattoes, mixtures of all types, racial and social, and even some white abolitionists—who were brought to Matanzas, the supposed center of conspiracy. Some time later, when the Commission had finished its awful work, more than four thousand people had been tried. The historian Vidal Morales y Morales, in *Iniciadores y primeros mártires de la revolución cubana* ([Havana, 1931], p. 297n), reports that of these, seventy-eight were condemned to death and about six hundred to prison; more than four hundred were exiled, and some three hundred died, presumably under the lash. Horrego Estuch, whose statistics on this score differ, adds that by the time of Plácido's death, the proceedings of the trial had covered almost one thousand legal pages.

---

[38] José de Jesús Márquez, *Plácido y los conspiradores de 1844* (Havana, 1894), p. 15; cf. Carruthers, p. 80; and Horrego Estuch (1960), p. 193.

In January, 1844, to quell an insurrection on the plantation of a French Basque, O'Donnell had the conspirators flogged on an *escalera*; thus originated the expression. But, like other aspects of the story of Plácido, this one, the exact means of torture, has been described in conflicting ways. Perhaps confessions were extracted by flogging the naked victim as he lay face down on a staircase; most likely, however, he was tied to a ladder. According to Emilio Blanchet, in the unnumbered pages of a special issue of *El Album* (Matanzas, June 28, 1904), devoted entirely to Plácido, "para lograr una confesión que cohonestase el preconcebido fallo, mandábase tender al presunto reo sobre una escalera de mano, atándole a ella y en sus descubiertas posaderas ensañábase el látigo, reforzado por alambres y sacudido por brazo vigoroso."

Two accusations, usually wrung by such torture, were sufficient, wrote Calcagno, for a person to be caught in the Commission's claws. He added that many Negroes, on learning that they were to be tried, committed suicide; they knew that their innocence was no protection and feared that the whip would extract names from them. There were, so Calcagno said, the cases of the son who was so crazed by pain that he denounced his own father, and the girl who informed on her two brothers, then, after becoming the mistress of one of the lawyers, went insane.

For many reasons Plácido was called to trial. General reasons include his prominence in colored society; prominent Negroes were the first to be arrested, for it was thought that they were sufficiently influential to have helped to organize revolts. Of course many of Plácido's poems seemed to contain thinly disguised expressions of sedition; Calcagno observed that all Cubans were familiar with, for instance, the "Juramento," "¡Habaneros, libertad!" and others, such as "A un cometa." The fact that the almost white poet married a Negress might have indicated that he sympathized with the Negroes or considered himself as belonging to their race. Though it has never been proved conclusively that he and Turnbull were close friends, Cuban authorities considered them so. And last but not least among these bits of circumstantial evidence were the mysterious trips inland and the arrests, especially the arrest in Villa Clara.

Naturally more specific charges were amassed against the poet. Indeed, thirty-two persons, probably many under torture, formally accused him of conspiracy. These accusations were varied. According to one, Plácido paid for a banquet at which rebel leaders agreed to recruit Negroes and to establish centers of conspiracy in key areas. At subsequent meetings the poet, presiding as "Viceroy," exhorted the members to exterminate all whites and, under penalty of death, keep the society's existence secret. The extermination was to begin after sufficient arms were assembled: members were to collect money to buy them and transport them along the Yumurí; and according to the accusation of the slave Tomás Adán, Plácido and others were to seize the militia's arsenal in Matanzas.[39]

The accusation which was the most serious and on which the indictments and sentences were based was that of a mulatto sergeant, José Erice. After testifying that Plácido, Turnbull, and their companions were members of a secret society that had been meeting in the home of a certain Jorge López in Matanzas, Erice committed suicide.[40] According to one authority, to substantiate Erice's claims, a strange flag was found in Plácido's possession when he was arrested, a flag thought to be that of the López society.[41]

Did Plácido, perhaps under torture, turn informer, too? Very few biographers suggest that he was taken to the *escalera,* but it was rumored that he escaped such a fate by betraying his fellow wretches.[42] Certain biographers, failing to produce really incriminating or unquestionably authentic documents, insist that Brigadier Salas treacherously advised Plácido that, in payment for freedom, he should furnish O'Donnell a list of friends involved

---

[39] *La Comisión Militar Ejecutiva y Permanente de la Isla de Cuba* (Havana: Academia de la Historia de Cuba, 1929), pp. 134-136; cf. Horrego Estuch (1960), p. 200.

[40] A part of this testimony is reproduced by Carruthers, pp. 85-87; it is reproduced in its entirety by Horrego Estuch (1960), pp. 340-352.

[41] Márquez, p. 15.

[42] One of the few to maintain that Plácido was flogged was the unreilable "F. U.," in "Plácido el mulato," *Revista de Teatros,* Madrid, September, 1844, no page numbers.

in abolitionist causes, and that the poet acceded to the request with a *revelación* containing fifty-five names.[43]

So sincere is most critics' admiration of the poet that they avoid reference to this shocking allegation; they believe it necessarily spurious, in view of Plácido's magnanimous character and the lack of documentary evidence. Others suggest that he momentarily weakened enough to agree to such a declaration, but then gathered the strength to refuse to sign it. Perhaps the whole story, like so many others relating to Plácido, is purely fictitious. Perhaps in this day of greater understanding of and sympathy for mental breakdowns, the effects of "brainwashing," and government torture chambers, one may reason that, if he did weaken, he was so crazed by fear that he was not responsible for his action, that it was no reflection on his basic character.

In prison Plácido received visits from his old and probably closest friend, Morales. In his biography, Morales quotes directly another dialogue that again seems too epigrammatic to be genuine, but in essence may be true. Plácido complained that although he had never hurt anyone, a secret enemy pursued him. Experience had taught him that being good was not enough; one must be lucky, too, and luck had never been his. Morales agreed, saying "y más segura es la sentencia cuando el hombre hace sombra. Entonces, si la envidia no lo persigue, la calumnia lo aniquila: el mal no está en el hombre, sino en su época, o en la índole de la sociedad que lo rodea." After several somewhat superficial reflections about life in general, Morales observed that the man passes from this world, but the poet is immortal. He then expressed regret that Plácido had not followed Heredia's advice to

---

[43] See Manuel Sanguily's reproduction of part of what might be Plácido's *revelación*, *El Figaro*, Havana, March 1902, and a curious sort of abstract of it by Vidal Morales y Morales, *Iniciadores y primeros mártires de la revolución cubana* (Havana, 1901), cited by Enrique Piñeyro, "Gabriel de la Concepción Valdés," in *Biografías americanas* (Paris, 1906), p. 353. More accessible is the 1931 edition (Havana) of Morales y Morales; see I, 311-312, 338-343. See also Sanguily, *Hojas Literarias*, III (Havana, 1894), p. 107; Francisco González del Valle, *La conspiración de la escalera*, Vol. I, *José de la Luz y Caballero* (Havana, 1925), p. 33; Carruthers, p. 83; and Juan J. Remos y Rubio, *Historia de la literatura cubana*, Vol. II, *Romanticismo* (Havana, 1945), pp. 8-9.

leave the Island. The mulatto replied: "Este amor tan entrañable que profeso a Cuba me hace olvidarlo todo: muchas veces he tenido arreglada mi maleta para emprender mi viaje, mas siempre me arrepiento porque aquí está mi madre, y por otro lado, creo que no podré vivir fuera de Cuba: soy muy criollo" (pp. xxx-xxxii).

It is rumored that Plácido had a third and last chance to escape his fate. Having refused the money to visit Martínez de la Rosa in Spain and to follow Heredia to Mexico, now, moved from La Vigía to the city prison, he was again offered the opportunity to become an exile. Three important friends hatched a plot to slip him from his cell to a boat leaving for some foreign land. The rumor, rather incredible, it seems now, had it that the poet refused, still protesting his innocence and believing that it would protect him.

Morales quotes Plácido's exhortation to the ten others, sentenced to die with him for the same crime, when they were being transferred to the prison (when they were being transferred to the death house, writes Horrego Estuch): "¡Compañeros, entremos al festín de las tumbas!" When his friend Santiago Pimienta —a rich property owner and the son of a lay priest—faltered, Plácido cried: "Animo; pues que somos inocentes, resignémonos con esta suerte: la posteridad nos indultará de esta injusta acusación" (p. xxxiv).

Early in the morning of June 27 Plácido and his companions got ready to be led from the prison to the death house in the military hospital of Santa Isabel. Their preparations are described in a rather touching way by "F. U.," writing in the unnumbered pages of the *Revista de Teatros* (Madrid, September 26, 1844). According to this account, Plácido said: "Esto ya está concluido; nos llevan a morir." He got dressed, then, noticing that one of the others was about to do the same, observed, "el viaje que vamos a hacer es corto, y pronto habitaremos otra región más caliente que ésta donde no se necesita ropa." As they stopped in the courtyard of Santa Isabel to hear their sentence, Plácido said: "Señores, ya estamos en el primer escalón del cadalso." When a soldier dropped the handcuffs he was preparing to put on one of the victims, Plácido remarked that "hasta los siervos se resisten a oprimir la inocencia."

Plácido consoled his companions by observing that it was better to go to the grave early in life rather than to reach a sad old age after much suffering; that now all that mattered was to approach death with courage and steadfastness; that others had been immortalized by dying bravely and his companions should emulate them; that he, Plácido, would die singing like a Cuban nightingale; and that, though creoles were treated like children and brought up like women, they died like men. When his friend Pimienta again panicked, Plácido composed a poem for him, of which only the following lines have been preserved:

> Abranse del corazón las anchas venas;
> Corra mi sangre a consolar tus penas.
> *(Revista de Teatros)*

Early the morning of the next day, June 28, the eleven, perhaps each accompanied by a priest, marched from the death house to the Cemetery of San Carlos in Matanzas. According to Guiteras, Plácido placed himself at the head of the procession. Morales reported that their hands were tied, but others say that Pimienta started to carry the large, heavy crucifix from the altar of the chapel in the death house. He chose this crucifix, since the parish priest, Manuel Francisco García, Plácido's old friend and confessor, had been able to collect only ten small ones, to distribute among the eleven prisoners. Plácido saw that Pimienta was too distraught to manage the large cross, so he exchanged with him.

García maintained that, as they passed a crowd of reputedly more than 20,000 spectators, Plácido recited what has become his most famous poem, "Plegaria a Dios," the end of which was drowned out by the rolling of drums. But, according to another eyewitness, Plácido's scribe, Manuel Gregorio Zambrana, the poet recited "A la fatalidad," the sonnet in which he indirectly referred bitterly to his mother:

> Ciega deidad que sin clemencia alguna
> De espinas al nacer me circuiste,
> Cual fuente clara, cuya margen viste
> Maguey silvestre y punzadora tuna;
> Entre el materno tálamo y la cuna
> El férreo muro del honor pusiste,

> Y acaso hasta las nubes me subiste
> Por verme descender desde la luna.
>   Sal de los antros del Averno obscuros,
> Sigue oprimiendo mi existir cuitado...
> Y si sucumbo a tus decretos duros,
>   Diré cómo el ejército cruzado
> Exclamó al divisar los rojos muros
> De la Santa Salem "Dios lo ha mandado."   (p. 36)

Upon reaching the place of execution, each of the eleven was blindfolded and stood in a wooden contraption with a headrest. To each were assigned four executioners, two to shoot at the head and two at the back. At this point Plácido is said to have cried: "Aplazo ante el juicio de Dios a mis verdugos y fiscales, Francisco Hernández Morejón y Ramón González." [44] The stories which circulated about these villains have been numerous and fantastic. According to one, as Hernández was dying of cancer, Plácido's colored friends gathered in front of the house to sing; their racket produced the Colonel's cry of repentance: "¡Plácido, perdóname!" [45] According to another, the poet had threatened that his ghost, in the form of an owl, would someday haunt one of the lawyers, perhaps Hernández. As he was dying a painful death, the delirious lawyer indeed thought he saw an owl alight at the foot of his bed (Morales, p. xxxiv).

All biographers, perhaps because they have all been moved by the dramatic implications, agree in essence as to the end of the story of Plácido, an end befitting a romantic hero. Some report that he cried: "¡Adiós, patria querida! A todos pido perdón y que rueguen por mí" (Horrego Estuch [1960] p. 249). All report that the first volley killed the other ten victims, but Plácido, only slightly wounded in the shoulder, rose in the smoke and pointed either to his temples or to his heart (on this score there is disagreement) and shouted: "¡Adiós, mundo! ¡No hay piedad para mí! ¡Fuego aquí!" [46] His executioners came closer for better aim. Morales added the final macabre touch: "El pueblo espantado ve volar por los aires aquella masa de una cabeza, toda poesía,

---

[44] Morales, p. xxxv; Horrego Estuch (1960), p. 249; etc.
[45] Horrego Estuch (1960), p. 259, etc.
[46] Morales, p. xxxv; Horrego Estuch (1960), p. 249, etc.

heroísmo e infortunio" (p. xxv). It is said that García separated the poet's mutilated body from the others and buried it apart, at the foot of the fifth pine to the left of the cemetery's entrance, a place later marked with a marble slab.

While imprisoned, Plácido continued to write, not only poetry, but a document or two. Guiteras and Piñeyro maintained that he sent his wife a short note, dated June 12; as far as she was concerned, it might seem to have been somewhat indiscreet, for his last thoughts were directed not only to her and to his mother, but to another love, Rafaela, too: "Alma mía. Adiós. Consuélate al menos el saber que mis últimos votos son por la paz y felicidad de Cuba y que mis postreros pensamientos se han partido con igualdad entre mi madre, Rafaela, y Gila." [47]

Because of some of the requests in the will, the original of which is kept in the Escribanía de Guerra in Matanzas, this document is even more surprising than the note. [48] After asking that his mother's ring be given to his wife, he cautioned Gila not to be overcome by grief, thereby closing the doors to heaven, the place in which he wished to find her—among those whom he loved. Following this fairly sane request are some which seem so extravagant that one wonders if indeed he had lost his reason: of García he requested that the ode of the pre-romantic Peninsular poet, Manuel José Quintana, be copied in gold letters from the funeral wreath of the Duquesa de Frías and be sent to Spain; and he asked to be remembered to the famous Spanish writers, Martínez de la Rosa, Juan Nicasio Gallego, and Zorrilla. Then he added, "no dejo expresiones a ningún amigo, porque sé que en el mundo no los hay," a remark which Figarola-Caneda thinks the poet made because anyone he called a friend would be suspect. He left eternal gratitude to his mother and wife, and to a person to whom critics avoid reference, since nothing is known about her—his sister, perhaps a close family friend or, more likely, a half-sister.

---

[47] This document, whose authenticity is questionable, is referred to by Piñeyro, p. 335, and reproduced by Guiteras (January 15), p. 23.

[48] Plácido's will is reproduced by Carruthers, pp. 256-257; by Horrego Estuch (1960), pp. 358-360; and by others.

Plácido is supposed to have written as many as five poems during this last imprisonment, five of his finest works. Horrego Estuch suggests that "Plegaria a Dios" and "A la fatalidad" were written in prison, while "Despedida a mi madre," "Adiós a mi lira," and "A la justicia" were composed during the twenty-four hours in the death house, the last poem being scribbled on the walls after Zambrana and the lawyer González temporarily removed his handcuffs (reports of this matter of restraint, handcuffing and tying the hands, are very conflicting):

>   En el alma, cual lucero
> Refulgente y peregrino,
> Tengo un retrato divino
> De la Deidad que venero.
>   En vano encontrar espero
> Esa belleza ideal,
> Y a la mansión celestial
> Ir a buscarla deseo
> Porque en la tierra no creo
> Que exista el original.   (p. 308)

Horrego Estuch believes the last of the five to be composed was "Adiós a mi lira":

>   No entre el polvo de inmunda bartolina
> Quede la lira que cantó inspirada
> De laureles empíreos coronada
> Las glorias de Isabel y de Cristina;
> La que brindó con gracia peregrina
> La "Siempreviva" al cisne de Granada
> No yazga en polvo, no, quede colgada
> Del árbol santo de la Cruz divina.
>   Omnipotente Ser, Dios poderoso,
> Admitidla, Señor, que si no ha sido
> El plectro celestial esclarecido
> Con que os ensalza un querubín glorioso,
> No es tampoco el laúd prostituido
> De un criminal perverso y sanguinoso.
> Vuestro fue su destello luminoso
> Vuestro será su postrimer sonido.
>   Vuestro será, Señor: no más canciones
> Profanas cantará mi estro fecundo.
> Mas ¡ay! me llevo en la cabeza un mundo,
> Un mundo de escarmiento y de ilusiones;

Un mundo muy distinto de este sueño,
De este sueño letárgico y profundo,
Antro quizá de un genio furibundo,
Sólo de llantos y amarguras dueño.
    Un mundo de pura gloria,
De justicia y de heroísmo,
Que no es dado a los profanos
Presentir: mundo divino,
Que los hombres no comprenden,
Que los ángeles han visto
Y aun con haberlo soñado
No lo comprendo yo mismo.
    Acaso entre breves horas
Cuando divise el empíreo
Prostrado ante vuestro trono
Veré mis sueños cumplidos;
Y entonces vueltos los ojos
A esta mansión de delitos,
Os daré infinitas gracias
Por haber de ella salido.
    En tanto, quede colgada
La causa de mi suplicio,
En un ramo sacrosanto
Del que hicisteis vos divino.
Adiós, mi lira: a Dios encomendada
Queda de hoy más: "adiós... yo te bendigo."
Por ti serena el ánima inspirada
Desprecia la crueldad de hado enemigo;
Los hombres te verán hoy consagrada.
Dios y mi último adiós quedan contigo,
Que entre Dios y la tumba no se miente.
Adiós, voy a morir... ¡Soy inocente!   (pp. 664-666)

Soon after Plácido's death, these five poems began to circulate in Cuba in unpublished form; some of them were published in Spain and the United States. It was not long before their authenticity, especially that of the "Plegaria" was doubted.[49] Won-

---

[49] Concerning its publication in *El Laberinto*, Madrid, August 16, 1844, pp. 278-279, see Garófalo Mesa, p. 208, and Francisco González del Valle, *¿Es de Plácido la Plegaria a Dios?* (Havana, 1923), p. 22. Carruthers, p. 102n, notes that it was published also in *Observador de Ultramar*, Madrid, August, 1844. It appeared, too, in the *Revista de Teatros*, Madrid, September 30, 1844, no page numbers, along with "A la justicia," "Adiós a mi lira," and "Despedida a mi madre," entitled "A su madre, despedida."

dering how Plácido could have been so prolific just before his execution, how the poems passed from his cell to print, and wondering if the scribe Zambrana was correct in maintaining that on the death march the poet recited "A la fatalidad" instead of the prayer, certain critics, particularly the "debunker" of Cuban literature, Manuel Sanguily, tried rather futilely to prove that "Plegaria a Dios" was spurious.[50]

Later, others became suspicious of the similarity between Plácido's prayer and the "Último pensamiento" by the Philippine martyr, José Rizal y Alonso (1861-96); but the similarity ends with the circumstances of the writing — both were composed by patriots, just before an unwarranted execution. Rizal's is a political, not a religious, poem, and was composed in 1896, too late to have influenced Plácido's work.[51] If there was any influence exerted, it was Plácido's on Rizal.

Was this a conspiracy of blacks against whites, or of creoles against Spain? Was there any conspiracy at all, or, as Hostos, Vidal Morales y Morales, and other historians have suggested, was this situation created and publicized by O'Donnell, who, by pretending to save the Island from a devastating insurrection, received bribe money in Cuba and gained prestige in Spain where he wanted to retire in easy and luxury? As more documents come to light, scant though they are, it seems that, if the Cuban slaves were not plotting to overthrow their Caucasian masters and rule the Island in the manner of the Haitian Negroes, at least they were plotting to gain their freedom.

Did Plácido help to lead the movement? This same scant material seems to indicate that he was indeed one of the leaders. But in view of what is known about his character and personality, it is hard to conceive of him as the power behind this or any other conspiracy. Apparently mercurial and temperamental, a "true poet" concerned with love and art, he would seem to lack the drive, stability, and cunning to direct a revolt. Rather than attempt to absolve Plácido of any complicity, as some scholars have done,

---

[50] *Hojas Literarias*, III, 113-114. See also GONZÁLEZ DEL VALLE, ¿*Es de Plácido la Plegaria a Dios?*; PIÑEYRO, p. 357; and CARRUTHERS, p. 241.

[51] See GONZÁLEZ DEL VALLE, ¿*Es de Plácido la Plegaria a Dios?*, p. 31; Garófalo Mesa, pp. 209-210; etc.

Hostos deliberately tried to attach it to him, for he believed it ennobled, instead of degraded, the poet's character: "No, gracias a la conciencia universal, no es inocente del sacrosanto delito de conspiración contra la tiranía el que así la detesta y así jura aniquilarla y así contrae el deber de combatirla y así verter su sangre generosa y verter la sangre maldecida del tirano" (p. 85).

North American Biographies

Soon after Plácido's execution, news of this Cuban *cause célèbre* reached not only other Spanish American countries, but Spain, France, Germany, England, and the United States. As Calcagno observed, "quizás ninguno, incluso los dos que acabamos de analizar [Heredia y Avellaneda] haya logrado más voga que Plácido, fuera de la tierra natal" (*Poetas de color,* p. 19). In view of the United States' traditional lack of interest in Spanish America, it is surprising the degree to which New Englanders and Carolinians were fascinated by Plácido, his life and works; this fascination is evidenced by the biographical sketches, reports of his death, and examples of his poetry, all published in English.

The nineteenth-century biographies in English constitute a special field of study in themselves. Some are remarkably accurate, are still referred to and quoted by students of Plácido, even by Cuban scholars, and are considered almost as primary source material. Of course others are so inaccurate as to be ludicrous, but historically they, too, are of value, for they bring to light the names and works of a group of early Hispanists who, though now forgotten, were, in their day, dedicated to the task of developing the first real North American interest in the Spanish worlds.

Incidentally, some of these works demonstrate how, a century ago, the North American press was inclined to distort the news from Cuba for purposes of sensationalism. As Richard Harding Davis commented in *Cuba in War Time:* "I had been kept sufficiently long in Key West to learn how large a proportion of Cuban news is manufactured on the piazzas of the hotels of that town and of Tampa by utterly irresponsible newspaper men who accept every rumor that finds its way across the gulf, and pass these rumors on to some of the New York papers as facts coming direct from the field" (p. 103).

The only detailed description in English of Plácido's appearance not only belongs in the category of ludicrous reporting, but ranks as some of the most absurd material relative to the poet ever to reach the United States. Strangely enough, it was written by a Cuban. It has been of great interest to students of Plácido and his period, however, for it has brought to light the identity of an intriguing, if scatterbrained, woman, whose path directly crossed the poet's.

Probably because she was born in Havana, although after eleven years of age she lived in Paris where she was to marry one of Napoleon's generals, the Countess Merlín (1788?-1852) considered herself an authority on all things Cuban. In 1840, when she was over fifty, she made a quick business trip back to the Island, where she was entertained royally by her aristocratic relatives and upper-crust Havana society. On returning to Paris, she published *La Havane* (Paris, 1844), a three-volume collection of inaccuracies and borrowings from Cuban critics; it contained also a passionate plea to O'Donnell to help out the beautiful, but unhappy, Island — a plea that fell, needless to say, on fallow ground. This remarkable work, a best seller in its day, was translated the same year into Spanish as *Viaje a la Habana*, with an introduction by none other than the world-renowned Cuban poetess, Gertrudis Gómez de Avellaneda, who, like the Countess, considered herself Cuban, although Europe was her adopted country.

The Countess' account of Plácido reached the United States via a very distinguished early Hispanist, once United States Minister to Spain, Alexander Hill Everett (1790-1847), and his review, published in Charleston's *Southern Quarterly Review* (VII [1845], 153-196), of *La Havane*.[52] Everett's translation from the Countess' French reads as follows: "The leader of the orchestra on these occasions, and the principal master of the revels, — the Straus [sic] of the Havana, — is the elegant negro Plácido. He composes

---

[52] FIGAROLA-CANEDA, p. 59, attributed this review to Everett. The attribution is correct, for the review, unsigned as was Hurlbert's article, was reprinted as "Havana" in Everett's *Critical and Miscellaneous Essays*, 2d series (Boston, 1846), pp. 325-380.

the airs himself, and nothing can be more original than his compositions, unless it be his costume, which is precisely that of the year 1798 in France. He wears a swallow-tail coat, yellow smallclothes tied at the knees with ribbands, silk stockings, and kid shoes with pink roses, and lace ruffles over his hands and breast" (p. 163).

So improbable is this description that one would automatically assume there was another Plácido, if it were not for the fact that Everett added the following: "This elegantly attired gentleman, is the same who figured as one of the leaders in the late conspiracy, and was recently executed at the Havana. He seems to have been a person of superior talent, and composed poetry as well as music. We have seen a sonnet which he wrote after being committed to prison" (p. 163).

Everett — who probably met the Countess when he was in Cuba on a confidential mission for the United States government the same year as she, 1840 — seconded her inaccuracies concerning Plácido, but was aware that her remarks were to be taken with a grain of salt, for he spoke of her volumes as "agreeable... with all their inaccuracies" (p. 153). That she took facts lightly, if it so suited her purpose, was confirmed also by William Henry Hurlbert. In his travel book, *Gan-Eden: or, Pictures of Cuba* (Boston, 1854; reprinted in London as *Pictures of Cuba*, 1855), he complained: "The Condesa de Merlin, an entertaining Cuban Scheherazade, who was by no means critical in her collation of authorities, once gave an account of the monteros, which resembled the reality of montero life and character, just about as closely as Mademoiselle de Scudéri's [sic] Persians resembled the friends and followers of the great Cyrus" ([1854], p. 171).

Though her description of the poet belies it, the Countess and Plácido must have known each other, perhaps meeting at a *tertulia*, for he wrote a poem in her honor. His ode "A María de las Mercedes Santa-Cruz y Montalvo, Condesa de Merlín," forced, artificial, and insincere, filled with clichés in vogue at the time, is typical of his and others' facile verse dedicated to people in high places. But, considering her own lack of sincerity, it was really more than she deserved. Plácido sang of her elegance, pointed out that she was Cuba's daughter, then concluded with a regret, probably not heartfelt, that she was leaving the Island to return to the greener pastures of Europe. But Cuba would remember her, he assured in the last stanza:

> ¡Vas a partir, y para siempre acaso!
> Vas a lucir del mar a la otra parte;
> Pero tu nombre en la cubana historia,
> Se esculpirá con letras diamantinas.
> Y que el hado nos veda contemplarte,
> Gozaremos al menos la memoria
> De tus mágicas gracias peregrinas,
> Y saboreando del placer la copa,
> Con noble orgullo contestar podremos
> A los artistas de la culta Europa:
> —Si al Ser supremo conceder no plugo
> A la patria dichosa de Varela;
> Un Virgilio, un Byron, ni un Víctor Hugo;
> Cuando el acento mágico resuena
> De la noble Merlín, y su laureada
> Frente se ostenta de atractivos llena,
> Ni al Támesis ni al Po debemos nada;
> Nada tenemos que envidiar al Sena. (pp. 623-624)

The most accurate, widely read, and complete of all nineteenth-century biographies in English was undoubtedly that of William Henry Hurlbert (1827-95), whose work is often referred to by Cuban scholars.[53] It formed part of the long and remarkably well-documented, though unsigned, article, "The Poetry of Spanish America," which, as noted previously, was published by the culture-conscious and intrepid *North American Review* in 1849. In this article Hurlbert proposed to present a side of Spanish American life "of nobler thoughts and higher aims than her politics have yet developed" (p. 131). He touched upon four Mexican and South American poets, but the greater part concerns Cuban bards, including Heredia, Milanés, Rafael María de Mendive (1821-86), and

---

[53] See WILLIAMS, I, 356n, 357n, for attribution of this article to Hurlbert. The fact that the same material was published in his travel book should remove any doubt as to the author; see LEAVITT, *Revue*, p. 133n. One of the earliest references to Hurlbert's article is found in Rollo Ogden's account of Spanish American poetry, an account published in the *Andover Review* (1890); see LEAVITT, *Revue*, p. 141.

especially Plácido, whom Hurlbert, in his other work about Cuba, *Gan-Eden*, called the "most interesting of the Cuban poets," noting that he "was not unknown in America by his *nom de plume* of Plácido" (p. 210).

The biography is relatively accurate; at least Hurlbert did not commit the blatant errors for which he criticized the Countess, except in minor instances: for example, he repeated the early mistake of assigning Plácido's birthplace to Matanzas; he referred to Turnbull as completely innocent of race agitation and spelled his name "Trumbull." It is complete to the extent that a bit of the political background is sketched in and essential facts are included: New England readers learned of the poet's rudimentary education and combmaking trade, of O'Donnell's cruelty and imprisonment of Negroes.

Hurlbert's account of the execution may be somewhat melodramatic, exaggerated, and misleading — especially with regard to Plácido's kneeling in the square and to the number of victims who accompanied him to the execution; but in comparison with many other reports, it is sober and reasonably exact:

> On the morning of the 28th, he was led out, with nineteen others to execution. He passed through the streets with the aid of a conqueror, walking with a serene face and an unwavering step, and chanting his "Prayer" with a calm, clear voice. When they reached the Plaza, he addressed his companions with words of brave and effectual consolation, and made all his preparations with undisturbed composure. He was to suffer first; and when the signal was given, he stepped into the square, and knelt with unbandaged eyes before the file of soldiers who were to execute the sentence. When the smoke of the first volley rolled away, it was seen that he had been merely wounded in the shoulder, and had fallen forward bleeding and agonized. An irrepressible murmur of pity and indignation ran through the assembled crowd; but Plácido, still self-possessed, slowly recovered his knees, and drawing up his form to its greatest height, exclaimed, in a broken voice, "Farewell, world, ever pitiless to me! Fire — here!" raising his hand to his temples. The last tones of his voice were lost in the report of the muskets, this time more mercifully aimed (*NAR*, p. 148).

Perhaps it is not to be wondered at that Hurlbert treated a subject so novel for the mid-nineteenth century, for he engaged in daring and unusual undertakings and, as one historian observed, was a "versatile" journalist.[54] His variety of interests is evidenced by his becoming an ardent Hispanophile — one of the surprisingly large group born in South Carolina. He was a bitter opponent of slavery and an active member of the abolitionist contingent in Boston; in 1861, on a trip back from New England to his native state, he was arrested and jailed for anti-slavery propaganda. Graduated from Harvard in 1847, he then entered that University's theological school and, after two years in Europe, became a Unitarian minister and hymn writer. Restless and adventurous, he traveled to Cuba and the West Indies; later he went to Mexico and, supposedly to escape a lawsuit, back to Europe where he died. After leaving the ministry, he showed himself to be a very competent writer, critic, editor, and correspondent for newspapers and magazines.

Through Hurlbert's copious footnotes, indicating the sources he utilized to write his biography of Plácido, one is led to other accounts, now hidden away in forgotten periodicals. For instance, he refers to a "short notice of Heredia, Milanes, and Placido, which appeared in the Harbinger for May 1, 1847, from the pen of an accomplished lady of Massachusetts" (*NAR*, p. 143n). This lady's brief account reads as follows: "His [Plácido's] deep-laid and almost barbarous schemes of revenge upon the oppressors of his race, which met with the penalty of a disgraceful and untimely death, have not destroyed the sympathy of the best hearts in his country and our own, for the victim of institutions which *breed* revenge; and his songs are on the lips and his name engraved upon the hearts of the noblest youths in his native Island. Placido was the poet of passion; Heredia of feeling, Milanes of reflection. They represent to us music, painting and sculpture."[55]

Farfetched though it is, her report is important for two reasons. First, by stating, after discussing Heredia and Milanés,

---

[54] MOTT, *A History of American Magazines*, Vol. II, *1850-1865* (Cambridge, Mass., 1938), 426.

[55] *The Harbinger*, IV (Boston, 1847), 322.

that she is turning to the "humbler though more well known name of Plácido," she confirms, as did Hurlbert, that the story of Plácido was familiar in the United States. Second, her words reveal the true cause of interest, on the part of the country to the north, in the Cuban poet. It seems that — though his poetry was appreciated, as evidenced by the many English translations — the real interest was motivated not by aesthetic values, but by abolitionists' concern over the mistreatment of Negroes.

Hurlbert's footnote leading to the most valuable material concerns a "large and very complete collection of the pieces published by him [Plácido] in the Matanzas Aurora," documents that Hurlbert says he was permitted to use. "This collection was made by Dr. Wurdeman [sic] of Columbia, South Carolina, a gentleman already favorably known to the literary world by his 'Notes on Cuba,' a review of which appeared in the London Quarterly Review for January, 1848.[56] Having relinquished the idea of publishing the volume, to the compilation of which he was led by his admiration of Plácido's genius, he has caused it to be deposited in the library of Harvard College" (NAR, p. 151n).[57]

Thus one is again confronted with that other Carolinian Hispanophile, J. G. F. Wurdemann. Although today very little is known about him, he was a physician, as perhaps can be deduced from the medical jargon he used in his *Notes on Cuba*, a travel book written at the urging of a better-known member of the Carolinian group, William Gilmore Simms (1806-70), and first published as a serial in *Magnolia* (March-June, 1843).[58] A death notice, printed in the *Charleston Courier* (May 8, 1849), concludes: "Dr. Wurdemann occupied a prominent position among the medical faculty — and it is not only in this character that his loss will be felt, but as a kind devoted son, and philanthropic gentleman, who has never failed to see and improve an opportunity to benefit his fellow man."

---

[56] There is no record of such an issue.

[57] This material is catalogued in the Harvard University Library as SAL 475.1.2. LEAVITT includes this scrapbook in his bibliography, *Hispano-American Literature in the United States* (Cambridge, Mass., 1832), p. 1.

[58] Unpublished correspondence between the two is preserved in the Manuscript Division, The New York Public Library, as "Miscellaneous Papers (Wurdemann Folder)."

Wurdemann's scrapbook includes a copy of a rare 1842 edition (Matanzas) of Plácido's verse, a copy bearing the signature of Henry Wadsworth Longfellow, to whom it may have originally belonged.[59] It is undoubtedly the copy used by Hurlbert, who lists this edition among his Spanish sources (NAR, p. 129). Inserted in it are newspaper clippings, containing poetry by Plácido and other Cubans, and, written on blank pages, are passages in Wurdemann's handwriting. Among them is the following brief account of Plácido's death: "Executed in 1844, in Matanzas, having been found guilty (through testimony extorted by torture) of being at the head of a conspiracy of the colored population to destroy the white inhabitants of the Island." This account and that in the *Revista de Teatros* are two of the few that maintain Plácido was tortured.

Other references by Wurdemann to Plácido include one found in the Carolinian's unpublished letter of January 6, 1845, written at the Cuban coffee plantation "Perseverancia" to his mentor, Simms; herein is provided intriguing news of what happened in Cuba the year after Plácido's death:

> By the bye, Plácido, the mulatto poet and leader of the intended insurrection (but who ever maintained that he was innocent) predicted a judgment from Heaven on the Island for the atrocities committed by the whites. It was a curious coincidence that the Hurricane, that swept over chiefly the very scenes of those atrocities, occured [sic] on the day of his patron saint and birth, San Placido. The general belief here, now is that the affair was much exaggerated in extent, and that very many innocent slaves and free negroes were sacrificed to the fears of the old Spaniards.[60]

Wurdemann has been the only biographer to refer to St. Placidus as the poet's patron saint; generally October 5, not March 18, is considered to be that saint's day. Perhaps the saint — rather

---

[59] CALCAGNO lists this edition in *Poetas de color*, p. 19, and in his *Diccionario*, p. 511; CORONADO also lists it, p. 9. GUITERAS (February 1), p. 43, and DE LA PUENTE, p. xxii, however, maintain that it did not appear until 1846.

[60] "Miscellaneous Papers (Wurdemann Folder)," The New York Public Library.

than the poet's calm demeanor, the pharmacist, or the hero of the French novel—is the origin of the pseudonymn. It is to be recalled, however, that Carruthers claimed that St. Gabriel—whose day, at one time, was indeed March 18—was Plácido's patron saint and the source for his Christian name. Wurdemann is also the only one to tell of Plácido's prediction of a judgment from heaven; (it seems—in view of this threat and the one to haunt his lawyer—that the poet had the habit of making dire predictions). The fact that Wurdemann was in Cuba at the time he wrote this letter—on the spot, so to speak—might lend credence to these two new pieces of information.

In the appendix to *Notes on Cuba* (pp. 355-359) is found Wurdemann's most detailed account of Plácido. Herein he stated that after writing the book, he spent another winter in Cuba, "that of 1833" (obviously a typographical error), when he learned about an "extensive conspiracy" in the area of Matanzas. He categorically maintained that Plácido was the leader and that Turnbull was "abusing the confidence reposed in him as an official agent of a government at peace with Spain" and was "plotting the destruction of her valuable colony." It is interesting to note that Wurdemann, as early as 1844, heard the aforementioned story, now accepted as true by modern critics, the story concerning the betrayal of the blacks by a woman slave: "The plot was disclosed by a negress slave to her master; those whom she denounced were arrested, and their confessions led to the detection of other conspirators."

Wurdemann's exaggerations are at times ludicrous. Concerning the trial in Matanzas, for instance, he wrote that "a thousand lashes were in many cases inflicted on a single negro." Startling is his explanation of what the Negroes, if successful in their revolt, intended to do to their enemies: "Many of the whites were to have been flayed and broiled while alive, and with the exception of the young women, reserved for a worse fate, all without discrimination of age or sex, were to have been massacred."

Despite the obituary, in the *Charleston Courier*, extolling Wurdemann's humanitarianism, he was not the humane Hispanist that Hurlbert was. Throughout this appendix he declares his opposition to manumission and intermarriage of the races; he writes, for instance, that "in whatever light it is viewed, one can only deplore the wild efforts of the abolitionist to force the freedom of the negro, which have only curtailed his privileges, and thwarted the measures employed by his master for his civilization." He urges Cuba to follow the system in the United States with respect to slavery; that is, instead of importing adult Africans, encourage procreation among the Negroes already enslaved, so that docility and discipline can be instilled in the new generation from the day of birth. In view of this arrogant attitude toward the black race, it is difficult to understand why the medico took an interest in Plácido.

A newspaper clipping in Wurdemann's scrapbook at Harvard leads to yet another account in English of Plácido. This clipping, containing a translation of "Plegaria a Dios," is entitled "From the Liberty Bell, Prayer, From the Spanish of Plácido, by Anne Warren Weston." It is a reprint, for the original in *The Liberty Bell* (Boston, 1845) is set in different type and, strangely enough, the author here figures as Maria Weston Chapman. Maria Weston (1806-85), married to Henry Grafton Chapman, was an active abolitionist in Boston and edited various anti-slavery journals, including, from 1839 to 1846, *The Liberty Bell*. The Wurdemann reprint bears a name more similar to that of her mother, Anne Bates, who married Warren Weston. Whether mother or daughter or both composed the translation, it is a good one.

In *The Liberty Bell* a brief biography of Plácido is included; it is filled with more sympathy for the poet than is Wurdemann's, for the ladies, like Hurlbert, were abolitionists. And once again is evidenced the fact that northern interest stemmed not so much from Plácido's artistry as from the cruel fate he and other Negroes suffered in Cuba. The ladies' ennobling of the poet is touching, although their mistaken facts are to be deplored:

> This noble being was publicly executed in Havana, in July last, on the charge of having attempted to free the slaves of Cuba. Himself a man of color and originally a slave, he wished to be the Spartacus, the Washington of his race. His heroic calmness as he emerged from the church, where, agreeably to the Spanish rites, he had been made to pass the twenty-four hours preceding the last, saluting his acquaintances and then chaunting in a loud

voice this sublime prayer, which he had just composed, produced an impression of the deepest regret on the throngs through which he passed to execution. The recital will make the American Abolitionists resolve anew, as at the commencement of their enterprise, to reject, and to entreat the oppressed to reject, physical force in their attempts to gain deliverance. (p. 67).

On a blank page of the 1842 edition of Plácido's poetry, Wurdemann jotted down a reference to a biographical sketch which appeared in a temperance journal, *The Christian Union* (VIII [New York, 1873], 62-63), a name later changed to *New Outlook*. The author, Amelia E. Barr, born in England, came to Texas with her husband in 1853. On his death fifteen years afterwards, Mrs. Barr and her daughters moved to New York where she earned a living by writing for the temperance journal and for others and by publishing some eighty books. Two additional abolitionists enter the picture here: Henry Ward Beecher and Harriet Beecher Stowe. Apparently they had suggested she come to the United States where they helped her market her writings. [61]

So fantastic is Mrs. Barr's biography that, as in the case of the Countess, one would conclude that there were two poets named Plácido. Actually, however, Barr's account is taken, without acknowledgment, from the autobiography "Life of the Negro Poet, Written by Himself, and Translated from the Spanish by R. R. M.," appearing in *Poems by a Slave in the Island of Cuba*, tr. R. R. Madden, M. D. (London, 1840), pp. 55-92. The autobiography is signed merely "Juan ————." In the preface, Madden adds further biographical data concerning the Negro poet and states that in 1838 a "gentleman at Havana" presented him with these poems written in Spanish by one whose name "for obvious reasons, I think it advisable not to publish," and whose manuscript "I have deposited... in the hands of the 'British and Foreign Anti-Slavery Society'" (pp. i, iii-iv).

"Juan," the poet whose autobiography and poems are thus translated into English and published by Madden, was Juan Francisco Manzano (1797-1854), the full-blooded Negro born into

---

[61] See LEAVITT, *Revue*, p. 141n.

slavery with whom Plácido was often confused. Since Madden did not publish the poet's full name, Barr jumped to the conclusion that the book concerned Plácido, whom she referred to as "Juan Placido." Thus she actually wrote or plagiarized the biography of Manzano, except for her concluding part concerning Plácido's death and the *Conspiración*, which she did not find in Madden's volume. Her explanation of these two matters is inimitable, containing some new twists, such as the fact that the "African Capatash, worth $60,000 in gold, plus much valuable real estate, perished in prison, either under torture or after it."

Fearing her readers might not understand Plácido's last words, which she gave as "Adios, Mundo!" she translated, "adieu, world." Her description of his death reads as follows: "As he sat down five balls entered his body. Amid the murmurs of the horror-struck people, he turned a face of supernatural light and courage on the shrinking soldiers, saying 'Have pity upon me. Fire here' (pointing to his heart). Even as he spoke two balls stilled the noble suffering heart forever. He was free at last. Death, the Liberator, gave him the citizenship of the skies."

In *The Black Man, His Antecedents, His Genius, and His Achievements* (New York, 1863), Williams Wells Brown (1816?-84) also confused the two poets and passed on the information that applies to Manzano, not to Plácido — that the Negro had been a slave until his freedom was bought by white friends, and that a white man sent the Spanish poems to England where they were published in translation. Like the majority of other Hispanists, Brown unquestioningly maintained that Plácido was a secret leader of the insurrection. His account of the execution is similar to Barr's — both seemed to know the exact number of bullets entering the poet's body, five, then two more which did the trick. Brown's new twist to the story was that Plácido asked for the dubious privilege of giving the signal to fire, a request that was granted.

Perhaps even more incredible than some of these English versions of Plácido's life is the actual life story of Brown. Born in Kentucky of a slave mother and a slaveholding father, he managed to escape to Lake Erie where he engaged in helping slaves flee to Canada by steamboat. After becoming involved in reform movements in Massachusetts, temperance, prison reform, and abolitionism, he was sent to Europe where he moved in distinguished literary circles that included Victor Hugo. Although in his many publications Brown treated various different fields, he became known primarily as an historian and outstanding authority on the Negro.

A more sober biographical sketch was written by Richard Henry Dana, Jr., in his *To Cuba and Back*. But he, too, stressed sensational aspects, thus proving once again that North Americans were fascinated by the brutality and racial conflict implicit in the story of Plácido, rather than by his artistic genius:

> The Plaza is in the usual style, — an enclosed garden, with walks: and in front is the Government House. In this spot, so fair and so still in the noon-day sun, some fourteen years ago, under the fire of the platoons of Spanish soldiers, fell the patriot and poet, one of the few popular poets of Cuba, Gabriel de la Concepcion Valdez [sic]. Charged with being the head of that concerted movement of the slaves for their freedom which struck such terror into Cuba, in 1844, he was convicted and ordered to be shot. At the first volley, as the story is told, he was only wounded. "Aim here!" said he, pointing to his head. Another volley, and it was all over.
>
> The name and story of Gabriel de la Conception [sic] Valdez are preserved by the historians and tourists of Cuba. He is best known, however, by the name of Plácido, that under which he wrote and published, than by his proper name. He was a man of genius and a man of valor, but — he was a mulatto! (pp. 100-101).

Among other nineteenth-century biographical notes in English which helped to spread the story of Plácido in the United States, Francisco Javier Vingut's *Gems of Spanish Poetry* (New York, 1855) might be mentioned. This slim volume is historically interesting, since it was one of the first attempts, with Spanish on one page and the English translation opposite, to publicize Spanish poetry in North America. But herein Vingut, who in Spanish published a fuller account of Plácido, merely states, incorrectly, that the poet was born in 1810 in Matanzas, and, correctly, that he died June 28, 1844 (p. 119).

Thus the writers who publicized Plácido in English belonged chiefly to two groups, the Carolinian Hispanist group and the

Boston abolitionists.[62] Hurlbert, a member of both groups, was conscientious and scholarly and consulted all the sources available to him, even sources in Spanish. The results of his efforts, written close to the time of the events, is now considered almost primary material. Wurdemann, a member of the first group, collected information in Cuba and possibly added new facts not culled even by Cuban scholars on the scene. Regretfully, some biographers, like the Westons, Barr, and Brown, confused Plácido with Manzano. The last two tended to romanticize and sensationalize their accounts for a romantic audience. In the Hispanic world, the United States press has long been criticized for this inclination to sensationalize, even to mislead deliberately, in the reporting of Spanish affairs; the tendency reputedly reached a climax with the yellow journalism associated with the coverage of the Spanish American War.

Fictional biographies

Plácido was the poet of the people. Even his "debunkers" admit that his appeal to the common man of Cuba, and to a degree of all the Spanish world, was unusually great. As Calcagno has noted, "quizás ningún otro en Cuba, incluso el mismo Heredia, haya obtenido en vida igual popularidad: las composiciones que rechazaba la censura, se multiplicaban por medio de copias manuscritas, y puede decirse que se publicaban sin imprimirse: ¿qué cubano de su época no se sabía de memoria los sonetos *A Celia, A la fatalidad, A Holofernes?*" (*Poetas de color*, p. 9).

After Plácido's death an effort was made to immortalize and ennoble him, to convert him into a romantic hero, a symbol of the liberation of a race or of resistance to Spanish tyranny. This effort is visible in some of the accounts in English, but also in the scholarly biographies in Spanish, wherein the authors are at times guilty of melodramatic passages, of stretching the facts, or

---

[62] See my brief mention of a few of these biographies in English, *Orígenes del hispanismo norteamericano*, pp. 99-110. Another short nineteenth-century reference to Plácido was made by M. M. Ramsey, in *Johnson's Universal Cyclopaedia* (1897); see Leavitt, *Revue*, p. 142.

distorting them. Some of these biographies occasionally approach very closely the admittedly fictionized works.

Today these fictionized versions, in which the author's imagination was free to soar, are of sociological and biographical interest, for written before or soon after his death, they reveal the various ways in which his contemporaries justified or condemned his behavior and the varying opinions they held of him. And they are of historical, if not literary, value, for they vividly illustrate Spanish America's somewhat primitive type of romantic novel and drama.

In 1843 Cirilo Villaverde (1812-94) published the novel *La peineta calada* in twenty-one installments, appearing in the newspaper *Faro Industrial de la Habana* (February-March). Involved with the insurrectionist Narciso López, Villaverde was arrested and imprisoned, but in 1849 escaped and fled to New York. He is now considered Cuba's outstanding novelist of customs, his best-known work being the classic *Cecilia Valdés* (1839; augmented edition, 1879).

In the less popular and successful novel dealing with Plácido, Villaverde's *costumbrista* technique is evident in the photographic descriptions of the story's sordid milieu and of the habits of the low-class characters. With its careful mention of actual streets, addresses, and areas in Havana, the book provides a map of the capital, much as Honoré de Balzac's novels provided a guide to Paris. But the plot is highly romantic. An implausible tale of intrigue and frustrated love is told, complete with an oversexed hero and a delicate, tearful heroine, frequent didactic asides to the reader, sinister figures, unexplained incidents, and "dramatic curtains" at the end of each installment.

As the story opens, the melancholy heroine Dolores appears distraught; she must be, reasons Villaverde, for her bosom is heaving. The reader soon learns that her distress results from the fact that husband Andrés has taken a mistress, the mulatto Rosario, whose face is more beautiful than her soul. Wife Dolores has somehow identified this mistress by spying in Andrés' shop an elaborately carved comb which she recognizes as his handwork. A gift to Rosario, it had been stolen from her by shadowy figures on the street, then recovered and sent here for repairs.

Careful descriptions are given of the home of Dolores and her mother, both of whom, on the father's death, came from Florida to Havana where they earn a meager living by selling candy and artificial flowers; supposedly they receive some financial help from Andrés, too. Andrés married Dolores after the debauchery of his youth was cut short by a year on a galley. Even more realistic descriptions are given of the home of Rosario and her Negro mother, a home to which Andrés began to stray a few months after marriage.

Rosario's mother Caridad, an *alcahueta* in the Spanish literary tradition, wants to marry her daughter to Andrés, but of course must first dispose of the wife. Caridad plots to have her kidnapped and murdered. The hired kidnapper decides he might as well rape her first, but Andrés arrives in the nick of time— although he no longer loves her, he balks at her being raped and killed.

At this point Villaverde abruptly terminates the exceedingly complicated plot. As if tired of the whole matter, he concludes with a few words to his *fiel lector* concerning the fate of each character. The kidnapper spends six months in prison, then murders his employer, Caridad. Dolores, exhausted by her husband's amorous adventures dies. Andrés seems reasonably sobered by her near rape and by her death. Rosario's fate is better; although she has lost the fickle Andrés, her *inocencia* is to serve her as a shield and guardian angel. Villaverde fails to explain how she so suddenly becomes so innocent and why she needs such protection.

Outwardly Andrés and Plácido share in common only their vocation, that of carvers of tortoise shell; no mention is made that Andrés shared Plácido's avocation of poetry. Andrés is depicted as white, however, and it is to be recalled that Plácido was light-skinned enough to have so passed. Of the personality traits conflictingly reported to have been the poet's, Villaverde gave his hero, Andrés, the sensual ones. Andrés' abandonment of his wife, for a mistress, might recall Plácido's abandonment of Gila—whether for the same reason is not known. If Andrés' character is meant to reflect Plácido's, then Villaverde interpreted the poet as a fickle, irresponsible youth, far too unstable to have plotted or led a revolt.

The Bolivian Joaquín de Lemoine (1857-1924) brought out in Santiago de Chile in 1875 a novel entitled *El mulato Plácido*.[63] This was the only novel he attempted; he went to Europe to live and to try his hand at other genres, a sensible decision, as any reader of this work will probably conclude. Set in Matanzas, the story concerns an outwardly respectable, but inwardly corrupt, couple: the husband is a gambler; the wife is strangely preoccupied by the young Gabriel, the faithful servant in charge of the children, Alberto and Berta. As time passes, Gabriel falls in love with Berta, but his only manifestation of this love is his nightly habit of tossing through her window bouquets to which are attached poems, signed "Plácido." He cannot declare his love openly, because he is a mulatto and because Berta's hand has been asked for by Arturo, a rich relative, who, newly arrived from Spain, is about to save the family from bankruptcy.

Disillusioned that his love cannot be consummated, Gabriel leaves the family and goes to Trinidad, center of the Negroes' subversive operations, to help out in an insurrection. The conspiracy is uncovered and a monstrous trial begins. To try to save Gabriel from execution, Berta and her mother rush to Trinidad, where, in Gabriel's prison cell, a scene of great emotion takes place. Gabriel finally declares his love and reveals that he is the poet Plácido. But now, for two additional reasons, his hopes are indeed doomed: he is soon to be executed, and, according to the mother's confession, he is Berta's half brother, fruit of her clandestine affair with a Negro barber.

Although as fantastic as Villaverde's, Lemoine's novel sticks closer to the facts of Plácido's life. The protagonist is a mulatto, was sired by a barber, was arrested in Trinidad, and took part in an insurrection. Of course the real Plácido was executed in Matanzas, not Trinidad. Furthermore, the personality as created

---

[63] HORREGO ESTUCH (1944), p. 148, gives the title of Lemoine's work as *Plácido* and the date as 1871; DE LA PUENTE, p. vii, gives the title as *Plácido el mulato* and the same date. But according to AUGUSTO GUZMÁN, in *Historia de la novela boliviana* (La Paz, 1938), pp. 77-83, containing biographical information and a summary of the novel, it was entitled *El mulato Plácido* and was published in 1875.

by Lemoine might well approximate the truth—a mixture of the vagabond and artist, cowardly on occasions, then courageous and rebellious on others.

The only play known to deal with Plácido was the one-act *La muerte de Plácido*, published in New York in 1875 by Diego Vicente Tejera (1848-1903). Tejera belonged to the generation of Cuban writers immediately following Plácido and, like him, achieved fame by attacking in patriotic verse the Spanish domination of the Island. Unlike Plácido, Tejera traveled extensively, to Puerto Rico, Venezuela, Europe, and to New York, where he wrote this ultra-romantic piece, containing many long, lugubrious monologues in verse, carried on by the innocent hero, victim of a cruel destiny over which he has no control. Other monologues, concerning the evils of mankind, are delivered by a priest, the only other character of importance.

The play concentrates on the last twenty-four hours of the poet's life, spent in the death house where he was supposed to have composed some of his most celebrated poems. Here in a room furnished with a large crucifix and little else, rough, unfeeling soldiers mill about drinking *aguardiente*. They discuss Plácido's forthcoming execution and decide to give him a line on which to improvise a *seguidilla*. The priest is shocked at the parody of justice and at the soldiers' levity. He declares that Plácido is being executed because "eres grande, y España no quiere grandes aquí" (p. 9). Thereupon Plácido recites "A la fatalidad."

Together the priest and the poet bemoan the fact that man is born unhappy; his earthly being is in permanent struggle with his divine spirit, so happiness is impossible to attain. Man pursues it, nevertheless; children seek it in games; young people, in romance; adults, in honors and success; and the old, in rest. Then the two proceed to a more specific source of unhappiness —the present tyranny, the whites' tyranny over the Negro and the Spaniards' over the Cuban. In both cases the despot is the Spaniard, and in both cases Plácido is destined to suffer, being both Negro and Cuban. At this point he launches into a recital of "El juramento."

Plácido protests complete innocence with regard to the *Cons-*

piración; he was tempted to join the rebel forces, he confesses, but fear stopped him. After this confession, he composes "Despedida a mi madre." Later, the priest joyously brings tidings of a strong possibility that the judges are now convinced of Plácido's blamelessness and that they have revoked the sentence. The poet's delight and relief are short-lived. Soon the rumor proves to be false, and the soldiers read the death sentence by which he is to be executed at five in the morning. Trying to adjust to this sudden turn of events, Plácido again resigns himself to death, and, as he marches across the stage, begins to recite "Plegaria a Dios."

Of all the fictional treatments of the theme, Tejera's probably comes closest to the facts. It deals with a specific point in Plácido's life and contains four of his poems, not all of them composed *en capilla*, however. Questionable of course is the depiction of him as completely innocent with respect to the conspiracy, but perhaps true is the implication that he was timid and fearful. And it is to be assumed that the false rumor of pardon was simply a device on the author's part to create suspense.

Thus in the fictionized works, the interpretations of Plácido's character vary as much as in the supposedly factual biographies. Villaverde saw him as a capricious Don Juan, completely devoid of leadership qualities. Lemoine, too, visualized him as weak, but on occasion, capable of great strength, great enough that when love was denied him he channeled his passion into revolutionary endeavors. Tejera depicted him as essentially a poet, too sensitive to become a militant rebel—somewhat as Horrego Estuch today interprets him. It is interesting to note that only Tejera stressed the artistic side of Plácido's nature; for romantic writers, the Don Juan or the political aspects of his life were far more intriguing. [64]

---

[64] A few other pieces of fiction based on Plácido's life are rumored to exist. According to Horrego Estuch (1944), p. 148, a Crescencio Rodríguez composed an *episodio histórico-dramático*. Both Horrego Estuch and De la Puente, p. vii, refer to a novel which was never published, "La Conspiración de la Escalera," by the Cuban poet and journalist Casimiro Delmonte (b. 1838). Horrego Estuch lists also a novel, *El mulato Plácido*, published in Spain in 1846 by a certain Larramendi; but according to De la Puente's letter to me of October 15, 1959, the author of this work was Agustín de Letamendi (1793-1854), writing under the name of Felipe José Torroba for the Madrid newspaper, *El Clamor Público*.

Chapter III

PLACIDO'S POETRY

Poetic talent

It was very difficult for a Cuban poet to achieve fame abroad, but to achieve it even within his own country was hard enough, for the competition has been keen—the Island has proved to be prolific in its output of first-rate bards. One major reason for this prolificacy is that the genre of poetry furnished an ideal outlet for Cubans longing to express their hatred of oppression. A poet could get his work through the censor whereas a novelist might not. A poem could appear innocent enough, but be filled with double meanings to which the censor was not able to object and which were clear to the public. As in opera, so in poetry, *libertad*, the word Tacón had objected to so strenuously, might easily be replaced by *lealtad*, which has the same number of syllables; the work was not damaged and the people knew exactly what was meant.[65] Since Cuba has practically always been oppressed, or so she has thought, political verse has abounded there.

Thus the history of much of Cuban poetry may be studied in direct relation with political developments. It is romantic poetry in the main, for as is often the case, romanticism in literature goes hand in hand with liberal and revolutionary thinking in political matters. Many of the most distinguished Cuban poets were, in line with various great Peninsular writers,

---

[65] Alfred Coester, *The Literary History of Spanish America*, 2d ed. (New York, 1938), p. 373; see also Hostos, pp. 12-13.

men of the sword as well as of the pen. Incidentally, because of their revolutionary activities, numerous Cuban bards have been forced to flee to New York where, even in the past century, forces were assembled to invade the Island.

By date Plácido belonged to the group of Cuban writers that flourished during Tacón's despotic rule. The group was led by the influential and affluent Domingo del Monte (1804-53), more a patron of the arts than a poet. He befriended Plácido, but preferred the cruder and more ungrammatical poetry of Manzano, "un lamento arrancado del corazón," and seemed to agree with Milanés that Plácido sold his soul for money. In *El Liceo de la Habana* (Havana, September 9, 1859), Del Monte observed that it was miserable to be born tan or black, but the degree of misery differed. At least Plácido was not a slave, and, although his educational opportunities were limited, they were far greater than Manzano's.[66]

Another leader of this literary coterie was Ignacio Valdés Machuca, whom Plácido in verse thanked for helping him to understand poetry. Valdés, likewise more a patron than a poet, had sponsored the publication of the *Aureola poética*, compiled after the celebration for Martínez de la Rosa, when the mulatto gained his first fame. It is said to have been Valdés who headed the movement to collect the money to buy Manzano's freedom. A final important leader of this circle was the poet Ramón Vélez Herrera, who, along with Valdés, helped to guide Plácido's studies. Vélez' volume of poetry in 1833 was the second published in Cuba, where printing began in 1787, the first being Valdés' *Ocios poéticos* (1819).

By style Plácido belonged to two related literary schools, romanticism and a Cuban brand of it, called the *siboney*. His work is romantic in its utilization of four of the major themes favored by romanticists: medieval legends, filled with pomp, ceremony, and artificiality; Moorish Spain, with its mixture of two cultures, the West and the exotic East; the "noble savage" of pre-Columbian America; and political freedom.

---

[66] Quoted by FIGAROLA-CANEDA, pp. 246-247.

For his most ambitious undertaking, the book-length *El hijo de maldición* (1843), Plácido devised a plot typically romantic in its implausibility and flowery descriptions of medieval trappings. The exact source for the story has never been determined. A *leyenda caballeresca,* perhaps in the mood of José Zorrilla, it is thought by some to bear faint resemblances to the legend of Hugo de Mataplana, a Catalan noble in the court of James the Conqueror and a dilletante who liked to bring home assorted literati and troubadours, to the story of the poet Ramón Vidal de Besalú, another Catalan living fifty years after Hugo, and to the classic incestuous plot of Phedra and Hippolitus.

In Plácido's epic, Hugo, face concealed by a helmet, returns to his castle after a crusade. There he confronts his impudent and imprudent son who, thinking his father dead, has taken over father's title and wife, Rosaura. Thereupon Hugo, sensing the domestic situation, delivers tyrades about tyrants; he has in mind his son, but probably Plácido was giving vent to his anger at Spanish despots in Cuba. Still disguised, Hugo tests his wife and son by singing, as he plays his jeweled lute, the lay of "el hijo de maldición." The lay concerns the knight Tristan, serving in the crusade of Godfrey the Great, during the reign of Pope Urban II; the mysterious disguised Tristan has committed a crime for which there is no pardon—incest. Upon finishing, Hugo explains to his family that the moral of his song is that whenever incestuous relations exist between mother and son, Tristan's terrible ghost will appear.

Meanwhile, Rujero, the castle's old retainer, suspecting that the helmeted knight is indeed Hugo, warns the son and advises him that his father can be identified by certain birthmarks; unfortunately the son has no opportunity to inspect his father so closely. But later during a joust between the two, Hugo reveals his identity. Thereupon Rosaura confesses to her husband that he has been poisoned; an antidote is found, but too late. The son dies from wounds inflicted while jousting with his father, and Rosaura, from grief. The castle burns down, and *Luzbel* enters with Tristan's terrible ghost chained to him. The retainer, turning out to be the troubadour Ramón Vidal de Besalú, lives on to sing the story to all who will listen.

Moorish Spain, a subject that fascinated even North American romanticists, such as Washington Irving, appealed to Plácido, too. An example of the Cuban's interest is "El bardo cautivo," thought to have been composed during his imprisonment in Trinidad. In this legend of the captive bard, shorter and less finished than *El hijo*, Plácido tells of the terrible tyranny of Tarfe, governor of Almería, whose reprehensible habits include persecuting Christians and jailing enemies. One of the latter is a young Moorish bard who, alone in a cell except for his only companion, a lute, sings of his beloved Granada and the injustice of Tarfe. (At this point one is reminded of Plácido, jailed in Trinidad by other tyrants.) In a dream the Moor foresees the surrender of his homeland to Fernando and Isabel, the death of the despotic governor at the hands of a young Spaniard, and the triumph of Christianity.

Suddenly the bard hears a crash, the collapse of his prison walls. Christians rush in and free the prisoners. The hero immediately asks to be baptized and to be allowed to fight Tarfe. The group hurries to the tyrant's castle, but finds he has sought sanctuary at the court of Fernando and Isabel. There, in a joust, Tarfe is killed by a page, the Spanish poet "Laso de la Vega." The young Moor, now a Christian, realizing his dream has come true, kisses the victorious poet's feet and gloats that the fate of political oppressors in the following:

> ¡Ay del mortal que sin razón oprima
> Al que ilumina inspiración suprema!
> Si lanza en él la maldición, se cumple
> Porque bajan del cielo sus sentencias.   (p. 82)

A third theme popular with romanticists of both North and South America was Rousseau's "noble savage," nobler than civilized man. In his *romance* "Cora," Plácido told the familiar story of the Peruvian sun goddess who, defying Incan laws, became pregnant. Her lover was a Spaniard, Alonso, who defected to the Indians because they were nobler than his countrymen. Cora is about to be burned alive by Manco Capac the Omnipotent, but Alonso arrives in time to save her. Then Alonso begs, at the feet of Prince Ataliba, that the old law of burning wayward vestal virgins be abolished. Ataliba, essentially a noble soul, agrees that his laws are old-fashioned, and all ends happily.

Plácido's most famous work dealing with the aboriginal theme is "El Jicotencal," a ballad that Menéndez y Pelayo praised highly. It concerns the Tlascala Indians, who withstood the forces of Hernán Cortés until finally siding with him to overthrow Moctezuma. They were "frank as they were fearless, and fair in their dealings," wrote William Hickling Prescott in his *History of the Conquest of Mexico* (1843), ennobling these Indians in the medium of history as Plácido did in poetry. [67] Of special interest to Plácido was the opportunity for lavish descriptions of elaborate costumes and trappings. Undoubtedly he was interested also in the underlying theme of liberty from oppression.

In Plácido's account, the young Jicotencal passes on his litter among Moctezuma's warriors, whom he has defeated. Then he jumps down and demands that they be released, not burned to death. He commands them to return to the capital and tell their chief that he, Jicotencal, does not indulge in the cruelty enjoyed by the Aztec ruler, nor does he stain the earth with the blood of captives. Moctezuma should be prepared for the day when Jicotencal's anger is really aroused, for the Tlascalan, with his spear, can dispatch three hundred of the Aztec's men any day; and if the bridges are destroyed, Jicotencal will build new ones with the skulls of the defeated! Then Plácido concludes wistfully that, since in this world nobody enjoys complete happiness, Jicotencal's luck ended and his death was sad—even the location of his grave is forgotten.

In the beginning of the ballad, the warrior's victorious appearance is heralded as follows:

> Dispersas van por los campos
> Las tropas de Moctezuma
> Lamentando de sus dioses
> El poco favor y ayuda.
> Mientras ceñida la frente
> De azules y blancas plumas,
> Sobre un palanquín de oro
> Que finas perlas dibujan,

---

[67] *History of the Conquest of Mexico* (Paris, 1844), I, Bk. III, 287.

> Tan brillantes, que la vista,
> Heridas del Sol, deslumbran,
> Entra glorioso en Tlascala
> El joven que de ellas triunfa.
> Himnos le dan de victoria,
> Y de aromas le perfuman
> Guerreros que le rodean,
> Y el pueblo que le circunda,
> A que contestan alegres
> Trescientas vírgenes puras:
> —Baldón y afrenta al vencido,
> Loor y gloria al que triunfa.—
> Hasta la espaciosa plaza
> Llega, donde le saludan
> Los ancianos senadores
> Y gracias mil le tributan.   (p. 144)

The fourth theme which Plácido shared with other members of the romantic *cénacle* was that of "down with tyrants and oppression." Because of censorship, he had to choose one of various devices: he could damn despots and praise freedom in medieval or past times, with backgrounds of the crusades, Moorish wars, or Indian splendor, as in the aforementioned works; or he could select settings offered by distant parts of the globe, as he did in "A Grecia," "A Polonia," and other poems; or, if dealing with the Cuba of his days, he could insert the cry for freedom very subtly, between the lines, as he did in "A un cometa," the first part of which is as follows:

> Cuerpo ignoto, que giras
> En la región del aire,
> Dejando tras tu curso
> Larga cola brillante,
> Tú, que por tantos siglos
> Corriste sin pararte
> Viendo generaciones
> Nacer y sepultarse,
> Tú, que entre tantos mundos
> Que en el espacio errantes
> Circulan, ves la tierra
> Mansión de llanto y sangre;
> Dime si has visto un pueblo,
> Do sólo un hombre se halle,
> Y ángeles obedezcan

>   Lo que su voz mande.
>   O por opuesto extremo,
>   Donde en paz perdurable,
>   Los vasallos sean hombres
>   Y el que gobierne, un ángel.   (p. 290)

Perhaps a second approach, when referring to Cuba, was that of indulging in flattery so blatant as to be derisive. Hostos criticized Plácido for writing poetry in honor of Isabel and María Cristina, on the occasions of their birthdays and saints' days, but Piñeyro maintained that this verse was written tongue-in-cheek, in derision. Carruthers concluded, however, that the poet, being "no fool," probably realized that the dyed-in-the-wool Spanish conservatives sided with Carlos, that Isabel and her mother, in comparison, were somewhat more liberal, the lesser of two evils; so Plácido's praise of these women might have been somewhat heartfelt (p. 39).

Other Cuban poets, such as Heredia and José Martí, attacked Spain's rulers openly, but it should be remembered that they did so from the safety of free countries. And occasionally Plácido, too, was open in his attacks—at least in his attacks on Don Carlos, as in the last lines of "El ángel de la gloria":

>   —¿Qué maléfica sed de sangre humana,
>   Ansia de ruines y ambición rastrera,
>   Mueve tu corazón, de tigre hircana,
>   A desolar, herir, matar doquiera?   (p. 642)

Plácido's poetry is romantic in style, as well as in content, in imitation of the style then in vogue on the Peninsula. Perhaps this imitation was not entirely deliberate, rather the result of a prodigious memory; whatever he read stayed in his mind and parts of it may have come out unconsciously as he began to compose. His "La partida del pirata," for instance, is very reminiscent of the vocabulary, tone, and spirit of José de Espronceda's "Canción del pirata." Critics point to many cases of borrowing. For example, Sanguily considers Plácido's "A mi amigo Antonio Abad Remos, en la muerte de Fela" as a "pobre y raquítica imitación de la que compuso Martínez de la Rosa a la muerte de la Duquesa de Frías" (p. 105). Figarola-Caneda points to passages in "A los natales de Delio" that recall Gallego's "Al dos de mayo." Parts of Plácido's "La malva azul," written on the occasion of Heredia's death, resemble work of the famous Renaissance poet, Fray Luis de León, who, although he did not live in the romantic period, demonstrated early romantic tendencies in his love of nature.

Plácido imitated not only Spanish romantic poets, but others as well — "imitó a cuanto autor estuvo a su alcance," as Sanguily put it (p. 101). A recent critic believes that Plácido, like many other Spanish American poets, was strongly influenced by Chateaubriand and the other French romanticists, whose works reached across the seas in Spanish translation — Plácido's "Atala" would serve as an excellent example.[68] And some of the poet's didactic verse, his many fables, for instance, probably reveal his interest in the Peninsular fabulists of the eighteenth century, Tomás Iriarte and Félix Samaniego.

Plácido is considered an early *siboneísta*, as well as a romantic.[69] Members of the *siboney* school, which reached maturity with José Fornaris (1827-90),. Juan Cristóbal Nápoles Fajardo (1829-62), Miguel Teurbe Tolón (1820-57), and the most distinguished, Joaquín Lorenzo Luaces (1826-67), endeavored to "Cubanize" poetry by describing Island scenery, by utilizing native themes, such as the cockfight and the pre-Columbian Indians, and by carrying on the peasant art of improvising verse at social gatherings. Of course, in turning to their native land for inspiration, they were essentially romanticists.

In at least four ways Plácido showed himself to be a precursor of this school. First, his habit of improvising verse at parties was *siboneísta* as well as Spanish. More important, his poetry contains three *siboney* themes: at various times, such as in "Al Yumurí," he refers to Cuban Indians, especially to the chief, Hatuey; his "Los dos gallos" and "El veguero" exemplify his interest in native pastimes and occupations; and, fascinated by nature, as Morales

---

[68] See EMILIO CARILLA, *El romanticismo en la América Hispánica* (Madrid, 1958).

[69] SAMUEL FEIJÓO, in "Sobre los movimientos por una poesía cubana hasta 1856," *Revista Cubana*, XXV (1949), 87, considers Plácido and Valdés Machuca the two most pronounced precursors of the *siboney* school.

pointed out, Plácido embellished his verse with motifs of native flora, as in "Flor de la cera."

Some critics believe that the "blossom poems" — not only "The Wax Flower," but the three companion pieces, concerning the blossoms of the cane, pineapple, and coffee — constitute the best not only of his *siboney* poetry, but of all his poetry. With these verses; light and delicate, yet subtly erotic, suggestive, and amusing, he created a new and delightful genre; they are far more original than his artificial poems of occasion or his heavy romantic efforts. Today, perhaps these emerge as the real *flores* of his poetic genius, those referred to in the humble epigraph printed in the frontispiece of many editions of his verse:

> Flores son de un ingenio sin cultura
> Cual las que dan los campos de mi patria,
> Ricas de olor, de tintes y hermosura. [70]

LA FLOR DEL CAFÉ

> Prendado estoy de una hermosa
> Por quien la vida daré
> Si me acoge cariñosa,
> Porque es cándida y preciosa
> *Como la flor del café.*
> Son sus ojos refulgentes,
> Grana en sus labios se ve,
> Y son sus menudos dientes,
> Blancos, parejos, lucientes,
> *Como la flor del café.*
> Una sola vez le hablé
> Y la dije: —¿Me amas, Flora?
> Y más cantares te haré,
> Que perlas llueve la aurora
> *Sobre la flor del café.*
> Ser fino y constante juro,
> De cumplirlo estoy seguro,
> Hasta morir te amaré;
> Porque mi pecho es tan puro,
> *Como la flor del café.*

---

[70] See, for example, *Poesías completas de Plácido* (Paris: Mme C. Schmitz e Hijo, 1862).

Ella contestó al momento:
—De un poeta el juramento
En mi vida creeré,
Porque se va con el viento
Como la flor del café... (pp. 478-479)

LA FLOR DE LA PIÑA

La fruta más bella
Que nace en las Indias,
La más estimada
De cuantos la miran,
Es la piña dulce
Que el néctar nos brinda
Más grato y sabroso
Que aquél en la antigua
Edad saborearon
Deidades olimpias;
Pero es más preciosa
La flor de la piña... (pp. 476-477)

Another of Plácido's delicate *letrillas*, "La calentura no está en la ropa," although not concerned with flowers, is equally amusing, with its colloquial, piquant quality, as seen in the following selection:

Lola, me dicen,
Volvióse zorra,
Porque su amante
Se fue con otra.
Digo que es falso,
Que la tal Lola
No había nacido
Para otra cosa;
Estaba en su alma
Ser voladora.
La calentura, etc.
Pretexta Nise
Que era una rosa;
Mas las viruelas
Y algunas otras
Enfermedades
Le han vuelto mona.
Mentira. Nise
Nunca fue otra.

Ni quince tuvo,
Ni ha sido hermosa.
La calentura, etc.
Dice Pedancio
Que en su edad corta
Hacer sabía
Muy buenas odas,
Lindos sonetos
Y amantes trovas;
Mas que los años
Todo lo roban:
Vaya a otra parte
Con esa bola.
La calentura, etc. (pp. 452-453).

Unpublished poems

Many of Plácido's poems are now lost. Those which he recited extemporaneously at parties were soon lost, unless perhaps an admirer copied them down. Many of those which the poet managed to have published in newspapers are gone forever, because a considerable number of these periodicals, or at least certain issues of them, have not been preserved in any library. Even some of the poems which were collected from newspapers and reprinted in book form are now unavailable, for several of the collections, issued in very limited editions, have completely disappeared.

The poems published in periodicals, but never reprinted in collections, are what Morales called *inéditos*. Figarola-Caneda, among other critics, objected to his use of the word; "uncollected" might be more appropriate. Morales had a point, however. He maintained that to all intents and purposes these works were inedited or unpublished, since they appeared only once in small-town newspapers of very limited circulation, perhaps with not even two hundred subscribers, and they seldom, if ever, reached outside their narrow confines.

Possibly an example of a poem lost because it was passed only in manuscript form is the following; it is included in the handwritten biography forming part of the Escoto material:

Cuando pasó Plácido a Matanzas había adquirido mucha popularidad por las brillantes composiciones a Isabel y a Cristina publicadas en la ciudad, y por la magnífica poesía que empieza:

> Cuando el poder con el poder combate
> Y [sic?] indeciso en su carro la victoria,
> Sobre ambos fija su mirar augusto,
> Y al fin sobre la frente del más justo
> Deja caer las palmas de la gloria,

composición que en los años del Gral. Tacón corrió manuscrita y que jamás hemos visto inclusa en la colección de sus versos.

Other examples of poems, virtually lost in their manuscript form, may be two brought to light in *El Tipógrafo* (Matanzas, January 26, 1902, p. 1) by a certain José G. Villa.[71] (Of course their publication in this little-known provincial periodical did not exactly assure them of worldwide attention; Morales would have considered them *inéditos*.) In his article "Gabriel de la Concepción Valdés," Villa speaks of Plácido's "flores de un día" which became "flores perdidas," unless someone wrote them down.

According to this biographer, one of Plácido's friends put in writing the following *décima* which the poet had improvised at a dinner party given by a planter, Irolas, on the occasion of his own birthday. The poem concerns Brazil's struggle for independence in 1821, when the Regent John VI was sent home to Portugal and his personable son, Pedro, took over the government. Reference is made also to the agitation in Spain being created by the Carlists:

> ¡Qué importa que en Portugal
> Haya una guerra civil
> Si don Pedro en el Brasil
> Hace su nombre inmortal!
> ¡Qué importa el cuadro fatal
> Que nos presenta Castilla:
> Que la gente de golilla
> Inquisición quiera a solas,
> Si en el cafetal de Irolas
> La paz y el contento brilla!

---

[71] A copy of this rare periodical is contained in the Escoto papers.

In explanation of the circumstances that led to the composition of the second extemporized poem which he saved from oblivion, Villa writes that soon after Rafaela's death, a friend discovered Plácido looking through a doorway at a dance. The friend approached and asked the poet why he did not enter. Plácido answered as follows, once again giving proof of his genuine grief, and the friend took down the words:

> Desde que el gusto perdí
> Vivo como en un desierto,
> Considerándome muerto
> Donde tan feliz viví.
> Si hoy tras la música fui
> No es buscando amante palma,
> Sino por gozarla en calma
> Y retirarme después,
> Porque la música es
> Un rico manjar del alma.

Concerning what Morales calls inedited works — works printed in insignificant newspapers and never reprinted in collections — it is to be noted that only part of Plácido's poetry published in the *Aurora* was included in the collection of 1838, generally considered the first; some, but not all of it, appeared in subsequent collections. Also missing may be some of the poems published in the *Eco de Villa Clara*, those which were not picked up in Morales' edition of 1886, as Garófalo Mesa points out. Many critics mention that Plácido wrote for *El Pasatiempo*, but they fail to specify what works appeared there and how many of them passed into collections.

One such lost poem recently came to light. It was discovered in *El Diario de Matanzas* (August 8, 1879) and bears the date March 19, 1839.[72] Where or how the editors of the *Diario*, forty

---

[72] A copy of this issue of the *Diario de Matanzas* is preserved in the Biblioteca Gener y Del Monte, Matanzas, Cuba. A clipping of the poem has been pasted in the cover of a collection owned by the Biblioteca Nacional de José Martí, Havana: *Poesías completas de Plácido* (Paris: Mme C. Denné Schmitz e Hijo, 1862). The poem has been reproduced in my "Una poesía desconocida de Plácido," *Revista Iberoamericana*, XXIV (1959), 363-366.

years later, found this "birthday poem" is a mystery. If the date is correct, it was written during Plácido's second residence in Matanzas, when he was supplying the *Aurora* with a poem per issue. It is an excellent example of a commissioned poem and one of Plácido's best efforts in this genre. All his poems of occasion are not to be "dismissed with a shrug of the shoulders," various critics have pointed out, because some of this work ranks with his best. [73]

The birthday poem illustrates how Plácido padded with meaningless, but euphonious metaphors, similes, and literary conceits. These seem to have flown facilely from his lips, but perhaps they were borrowed or invented beforehand, then stored in his mind for later use. At any rate, they indicate an inherent creative power that was wonderfully well-developed for so young and uneducated a person. The ornate, sentimental style reflects the influence of Spanish romantic poets. The meter is that of an irregular *silva*, a form which Plácido frequently used in fables, odes, and laudatory poems. Dedicated to "D. José Florencio García," the first two of the four stanzas are as follows:

> Ya el caracol sonante
> Que ufano tañe entre la mar sombría
> El incansable pescador, la fría
> Serena faz del alba fulgurante
> Que de aljófar partículas rocía
> Y el gorjear del ruiseñor amante,
> La vuelta anuncian de tu fausto día.
>   Salud, Florencio: tu pasada vida
> Inmaculada fue, luciente y pura
> Como el sol tropical; la frente erguida
> Alzar puedes cual palma en la llanura;
> Que quien de un padre las cenizas honra
> Y a costa de sudores y fatigas
> Los créditos cubriendo su honor salva,
> Justo será que el cielo le bendiga.
> Y cuando el hado su existir sucumba,
> A sus hijos legando tal ejemplo,
> Ellos dirán llorosos en su tumba:
> —*Gloria es su nombre, su memoria un templo.*

---

[73] CARRUTHERS, p. 197; see also FIGAROLA-CANEDA, p. 95.

Thanks to a complete set of the *Pasatiempo* (printed in Matanzas for a year, then in Havana) in the private library of De la Puente, the problem of what Plácido published in that periodical, and when, is now solved. In issues dating from May 10 to September 2, 1834, six poems appear. The first, honoring Manuel González del Valle ("Dorilo," or possibly for purposes of rhyme, "Dorila"), was thus published nine days after the festival, held on the banks of the Almendares River, for Martínez de la Rosa. This "Octava" could be called inedited, in Morales' sense of the word; that is, probably it has appeared only once, in a provincial newspaper, and has not been picked up in collections. Since copies of the periodical are indeed scarce, the poem might easily have become one of Plácido's "lost" works:

¿Ves cuando el alba con copioso lloro
Argenta de Almendar las bellas flores,
Hacerle salva en apacible coro
Los canarios y arpados ruiseñores?
Pues yo a Dorila con mi lira de oro
Quiero loar en cánticos mayores;
Que si el alba al nacer perlas destila,
Diamantes da la frente de Dorila.   (May 10, 1834)

The second, a sonnet entitled "A Castalia," was reprinted by Morales in his collection of 1886 (p. 1) as "Invocación." Here indeed is proof of the truth of the accusations, made by Figarola-Caneda and others, that Morales radically changed Plácido's originals. The editor and botanist changed Plácido's fourth line to "Siempre acogido con amor ardiente"; his eighth line to "Hace mi fácil numen elocuente"; and his twelfth line to "Y así, mundo, si estoy equivocado":

Fuente Castalia, donde solamente
Basta probar tus aguas cristalinas
Para ser de las musas peregrinas
El poseedor feliz eternamente.
Dame tus aguas, ¡oh Castalia fuente!
Y verás qué pinturas tan divinas,
Tan sencillas, tan claras y tan finas
Hago desde el ocaso hasta el oriente.
Pero si acaso a la plegaria mía
De tus aguas el curso has enfrenado,

No por eso acibarás mi alegría.
Y así, lector, si estoy equivocado,
Bien puedes perdonar; pues todavía
De Castalia las aguas no he probado.
(June 3, 1834)

The third work, another sonnet, "A un amigo en sus días," fails to appear in collections; Morales would consider it unpublished:

Suena la Fama su clarín, y luego
Sus alas tiende el céfiro en las flores,
Dando a los bosques, prados y pastores
Salud y vida y abundante riego.
   A Ceres sigue con sagaz sosiego
Alado coro de áulicos cantores,
Que el nombre tuyo llevan con loores
Del clima helado a la región del fuego.
   Pero le resta más solemne palma,
Que es la grata emoción y la alegría
Con que tu amigo fiel te brinda el alma.
   Y toda su familia en compañía
Al cielo ruego que en serena calma
Mil años cuentes de tu santo el día. (June 7, 1834)

The *letrilla* about the January moon is almost as charming as the blossom poems. It has been reproduced frequently, by Morales (pp. 451-452) and others, without indication of where or when it first appeared. In this case Morales limited himself to omitting the eleventh line and the last stanza and to changing a word here and there. It begins as follows:

Resuene el pandero,
Al monte, a la loma,
Pastores, que asoma
La luna de enero.
   No la estéis buscando
Sobre el firmamento,
Que viene cual viento
Las flores hollando.
¡Si al ver el salero
De mi pastorcilla
Y el rostro hechicero,
Parece que brilla
La luna de enero! (June 10, 1834)

The fifth and sixth of Plácido's poems published in the *Pasatiempo* are of biographical interest, because of their references to Rafaela. In the fifth, "Epístola," as evidenced in the following first half of the work, he states that her greatest virtues were serenity, modesty, and fidelity. He alludes to her death by cholera and intimates that his sorrow was so acute that he was led to the brink of suicide. Interesting, too, is this poem's resemblance to "A mi amigo Antonio Abad Remos," reproduced by Morales (pp. 523-525). Although the two works are similar in subject matter and tone and although certain lines are identical, Morales' version is quite different. Perhaps two distinct poems were composed or perhaps here Morales did a very thorough job of rewriting:

> Desde los bordes del sepulcro helado...
> Lloré, me entristecí y algunas veces
> Atentar contra mí quise yo mismo.
> (Tanto puede una eleve, que al más cuerdo
> Hará que pierda la virtud y el juicio.)
> Empero plugo al cielo consolarme
> Habiendo el rostro de las gracias visto:
> Era el de Fela, dulce y linda joven
> Cual jamás vieron de Colón los hijos.
> La quietud, la modestia y la constancia
> Eran sus más preciosos atractivos
> (Prendas bien raras en la edad presente
> Merecedoras del mejor destino).
> Todas las flores del amor gozaba,
> Cuando el terrible y fiero torbellino
> Del cólera horroroso, a desolarnos
> Cruzando el mar del septentrión nos vino.
> Aun me atreví a esperar que el santo cielo
> En mí mostrara su bondad benigna;
> Pero he nacido, Abad, muy desgraciado:
> Perder mi único bien era preciso...
> Ella ha muerto a mi vista, y breve tiempo
> Tardaré para hallarla en el Elíseo.   (June 30, 1834)

The sixth work, "El desdén," an ode surprisingly enough reproduced by Morales without any changes whatsoever, is of interest for at least two reasons. First of all, the seventh through tenth lines might indicate that even by this early date Plácido was aware that his life was to be short. Secondly, it shows the lengths to which his eroticism and sensuality might have gone; herein is implied that his affair with Rafaela was consummated — with the aid of wine, which, according to Morales, the poet never touched. These themes of the shortness of life and unrestrained physical passion seem to combine into the stereotyped philosophy of "Gather ye rosebuds while ye may."

>Ven, mitad de mi alma;
>Ven, mi dulce morena,
>Y orna mi frente y tirso
>De pámpanos y yedra.
>¡Ay! no en sanos desdenes
>Las gratas horas pierdas;
>Quizá no están muy lejos
>Las desdichas acerbas
>Con que el mortal sañuda
>La parca dura acecha.
>Ven, morena, a mis brazos,
>Y disfrutar me deja
>Los deleitosos días
>Que de vivir nos restan.
>Deja besar tus ojos,
>Y tu boca hechicera,
>Y tu bella garganta
>Y tus... sí, llega, llega.
>Pero antes echa vino
>En esa copa; echa
>Hasta que se rebose...
>Basta ya; prueba, prueba.
>¡Qué dulce! ¡qué sabroso!
>¿No es verdad? Dime, Fela,
>¿No sientes inflamarse
>Tu pecho en llama nueva?
>¿No te embelesa el gusto?
>¡Oh, cómo centellean
>Tus ojos! ¡Si parece
>Tu cuerpo de candela!
>¡Qué! ¿La apuraste toda?
>Pues bien, dame otra llena.
>¡Ah!, ¡qué sabroso y suave!
>Mas... suelta la botella,
>Que ya de amor discurre
>Fuego activo en mis venas.
>Abrázame, alma mía.
>Estrecha más..., estrecha.
>Más que el dulce, son dulces

> Tus labios, mi morena,
> Y tu cuerpo, y tus brazos
> Y toda tú, mi Fela.
> Abrázame, ¡ay!, abrázame,
> Y deja que me muera.   (September 2, 1834)

North American Translations

Although undoubtedly nineteenth-century readers in the United States were more intrigued by the sensational aspects of Plácido's life than by the artistic merits of his poetry, most of their biographical accounts included a bit of verse in English translation. As might be expected, the favorite work was "Plegaria a Dios," probably because of its religious fervor and the dramatic events associated with it — it was composed *en capilla* just before execution, probably recited by the author on his death march, and then smuggled out of prison to circulate in Havana and even Madrid. The English version that has been most frequently reproduced in the United States is that of Hurlbert, who, with his "The Poetry of Spanish America" and *Gan-Eden*, contributed more than any other Hispanophile in arousing North American interest in Plácido.

PRAYER TO GOD

> O God of love unbounded! Lord supreme!
>   In overwhelming grief, to thee I fly;
>   Rending this veil of hateful calumny,
> O, let thine arm of might my fame redeem!
>   Wipe thou this foul disgrace from off my brow,
>   With which the world hath sought to stamp it now.
>
> Thou King of kings, my fathers' God and mine,
>   Thou only art my sure and strong defence;
>   The polar snows, the tropic fires intense,
> The shaded sea, the air, the light, are thine;
>   The life of leaves, the water's changeful tide,
>   All things are thine, and by thy will abide.
>
> Thou art all power; all life from thee goes forth,
>   And fails or flows obedient to thy breath;
>   Without thee, all is naught, in endless death
> All nature sinks, forlorn and nothing worth.
>   Yet even the void obeys thee, and from naught,

By thy dread word, the living man was wrought.

Merciful God! how should I thee deceive?
   Let thy eternal wisdom search my soul!
   Bowed down to earth by falsehood's base control,
Her stainless wings not now the air may cleave.
   Send forth thine hosts of truth, and set her free!
   Stay thou, O Lord! the oppressor's victory.

Forbid it, Lord, by that most free outpouring
   Of thine own precious blood for every brother
   Of our lost race, and by thy Holy Mother,
So full of grief, so loving, so adoring,
   Who, clothed in sorrow, followed thee afar,
   Weeping thy death like a declining star.

But if this lot thy love ordains to me, —
   To yield to foes most cruel and unjust,
   To die, and leave my poor and senseless dust
The scoff and sport of their weak enmity,—
   Speak, thou! and then thy purposes fulfil;
Lord of my life, work thou thy perfect will!
(*NAR*, pp. 146-147; *Gan-Eden*, pp. 213-214)

Perhaps because Hurlbert's article was unsigned, the anthologists of Spanish poetry in English translation have failed to give him credit; few indicate even the place of publication.[74] Cuban authorities lead one to the correct place, but the wrong translator. In *Poetas de color*, Calcagno states: "La plegaria fue también muy bien interpretada por Longfellow, traducción que apareció en North American Review, Boston, tomo 68, pág. 129 y siguientes en un opúsculo sobre poetas cubanos, vidas y caracteres, según datos que creemos suministró el Sr. Guiteras de Matanzas" (p.

---

[74] THOMAS WALSH includes the "Plegaria" in *Hispanic Anthology* (New York, 1920), calling the translator "Anonymous," p. 433; and in his *The Catholic Anthology* (New York, 1939), with the omission of the last two lines of the first stanza, as "Anonymous Translation from the Spanish," p. 257. COESTER, in *The Literary History of Spanish America*, includes it with no mention of the translator, pp. 389-390. The only one to guide the reader to the correct place of publication, though not the translator, is Francisco Javier Vingut, who, omitting the fifth stanza, reproduces it in his *Gems of Spanish Poetry* (New York, 1855), crediting merely the "N. A. Review," p. 119.

19n). [75] Figarola-Caneda also attributed this translation to Longfellow (p. 96).

At least three reasons can be offered for assuming that Hurlbert himself translated the "Plegaria" into English. [76] First, by publishing it without acknowledgments, as he did in the *Review* and in *Gan-Eden,* he thereby claimed it as his own. [77] And he seems to have been ethical, since in the case of certain translations of Heredia, included in the same article, he scrupulously gave credit to others. [78] Secondly, he stated that he himself translated various other works of Heredia; thus he was capable of translating from Spanish, and there is no reason to suspect that he did not translate Plácido's work, too. [79] Thirdly, a paternal note might be detected in his presentation of "Prayer to God": "It is difficult to convey into English words the fire and force of expression of this noble poem; but we trust that the following version does not wholly misrepresent it" (*NAR,* p. 146).

Available to Hurlbert were other translations, but a glance at them shows that he did not copy. In the Wurdemann scrapbook in Hurlbert's possession is a clipping prefaced as follows in the former's handwriting: "While under condemnation, 'Placido' was

---

[75] Of the three Guiteras brothers born in Matanzas, Antonio, Eusebio, and Pedro José, whom Calcagno lists in his *Diccionario,* the one indicated must have been the last-named, author of the frequently mentioned biography of Plácido published in *El Mundo Nuevo.*

[76] That Hurlbert's knowledge of Spanish was more than rudimentary is evidenced not only by his excellent translations, but by remarks of a linguistic nature throughout the article, such as his discussion of elision in the "negro Spanish of Cuba," *NAR,* p. 157n. In preserved correspondence, however, he makes no reference to these matters; see the William M. Evarts Papers and William Collins Whitney Papers, The Library of Congress.

[77] LEAVITT, *Revue,* p. 136, writes that the chapter about Plácido in *Gan-Eden* was reprinted in *Chamber's Journal* (October 22, 1859) and in *Littell's Living Age* (January 7, 1860).

[78] Hurlbert credited James Kennedy, "H. B. M.'s Judge in the Mixed Court" of Havana for publishing in 1844 selections from Heredia's work, with translations, *NAR,* p. 139n. And "most of our readers we trust are acquainted with his [Heredia's] poem, 'Niagara,' a fine version of which by Bryant is to be found in Mr. Longfellow's 'Poets and Poetry of Europe'," *NAR,* p. 140n.

[79] "We have translated several other poems of Heredia, wholly or in part, which our limits forbid us to insert in this article." Then follows a translation of "La estación de los nortes," which Hurlbert claims as his own, "a version as we have been able to make of it," *NAR,* p. 140.

visited by some gentlemen, one of whom expressed a doubt of his poetical powers. He sat down and wrote the prayer, of which the following is a literal (though not poetical) translation." This humble acknowledgment of lack of artistry might indicate that the author of his version was Wurdemann himself; perhaps it was to form part of the English edition, which, according to Hurlbert's footnote, Wurdemann was contemplating:

PRAYER TO GOD

FROM THE SPANISH OF PLACIDO, A PRISONER IN THE MATANZAS PRISON

Being of love unbounded! mighty God!
In overwhelming grief to thee I fly.
Extend thy hand omnipotent, and rend
From this base calumny the odious veil;
Tear thou away the ignominious seal,
With which the world now seeks to brand my brow.
Thou King of kings! God of my ancestors,
And mine! Thou art my sole defender, Lord!
All things obey Thee. The dark sea, its waves
And finny tribes, the daylight of the skies,
The ambient air, the southern fires and the
Northern snows, the life of plants, the rivers'
Ebb and flow, hang upon thy will alone.
Thou hast all power; Thou canst them destroy
And by thy sacred breath again restore.
Deprived of Thee the whole sinks into nought,
Lost in the deep eternity of Time.
Yet even void obeys thee, for, out of
Nothing, all mankind thou didst create.
I cannot deceive Thee: God of mercy!
Let thy eternal wisdom search my soul.
In oppress'd innocence, from the free air
Restrained, by calumny most foul her wings
Are closed. Still, if to Thee seem good that I,
By cruel malice now shall die; and, to
Feast malignant joys, my cold remains to
Outrage be resigned, then speak—, take thou this
Life, and in me thy will fulfil, my God!

Also available to Hurlbert was another translation in the Wurdemann scrapbook, the Westons', reprinted from *The Liberty*

Bell. The original, published as follows in that journal, is prefaced by their biography of Plácido, the poem in Spanish, and by the remark: "The translation gives nearly the literal meaning; but our language hardly affords the means of doing justice to the 'long low-rolling knell' of the Spanish":

PRAYER

FROM THE SPANISH OF PLACIDO

Being of infinite goodness! God Almighty!
    I hasten in mine agony to thee!
    Rending the hateful veil of calumny,
Stretch forth thine arm omnipotent in pity!
    Efface this ignominy from my brow
    Wherewith the world is fain to brand it now!

Oh King of kings! thou God of my forefathers!
    My God! thou only my defence shalt be,
    Who gav'st her riches to the shadowed sea;
From whom the North her frosty treasure gathers,—
    Of heavenly light and solar flame the giver,
    Life to the leaves, and motion to the river.

Thou canst do all things. What thy will doth cherish
    Revives to being at thy sacred voice.
    Without Thee all is naught, and at thy choice
In fathomless eternity must perish.
    Yet e'en that nothingness thy will obeyed,
    When of its void humanity was made.

Merciful God! I can deceive thee never;
    Since, as through ether's bright transparency,
    Eternal wisdom still my soul can see
Through every earthly lineament forever.
    Forbid it, then, that Innocence should stand
    Humbled, while Slander clasps her impious hand.

But it the lot thy sovereign power shall measure
    Must be to perish as a wretch accursed,
    And men shall trample over my cold dust,—
The corse outraging with malignant pleasure,
    Speak and recal my being at thy nod!
    Accomplish in me all thy will, my God!   (pp. 70-71)

PLACIDO'S POETRY

Although these two English versions were in Hurlbert's possession, he must have consulted Spanish sources, for he included, as the fifth of six sextets, a stanza not found in the work of Wurdemann and the Westons.[80] This fact helps to settle the dispute concerning the Spanish original as published in Morales' collection. Critics object particularly to Morales' inclusion of the same fifth sextet, plus an octave placed before it. Since the sextet, though not the octave, appear in Hurlbert's translation of 1849, the former could not have been invented by Morales in 1886, but the latter, standing out awkwardly amid the sextets, probably in spurious.

  Ser de inmensa bondad, Dios poderoso,
A vos acudo en mi dolor vehemente;
Extended vuestro brazo omnipotente,
Rasgad de la calumnia el velo odioso
Y arrancad este sello ignominioso
Con que el mundo manchar quiere mi frente.
  Rey de los reyes, Dios de mis abuelos,
Vos sólo sois mi defensor, Dios mío;
Todo lo puede quien al mar sombrío
Olas y peces dio, luz a los cielos,
Fuego al Sol, giro al aire, al Norte hielos,
Vida a las plantas, movimiento al río.
  Todo lo podéis vos; todo fenece
O se reanima a vuestra voz sagrada:
Fuera de vos, Señor, el todo es nada
Que en la insondable eternidad perece,
Y aun esa misma nada os obedece;
Pues de ella fue la humanidad creada.
  Yo no os puedo engañar, Dios de clemencia;
Y pues vuestra eternal sabiduría
Ve al través de mi cuerpo el alma mía
Cual del aire a la clara transparencia,
Estorbad que humillada la inocencia
Bata sus palmas la calumnia impía.
  Estorbadlo, Señor, por la preciosa
Sangre vertida, que la culpa sella

---

[80] His Spanish sources had to include more than the collection of Plácido's poetry dated 1842 (but perhaps not published until 1846), which Hurlbert referred to and which is included in the Wurdemann scrapbook, "Poems of Gabriel de la Concepción Valdés," SAL 475.1.2, Harvard University Library, for this edition does not contain the "Plegaria."

> Del pecado de Adán o por aquella
> Madre cándida, dulce y amorosa,
> Cuando envuelta en pesar, mustia y llorosa
> Siguió tu muerte como helíaca estrella.
>   Por aquella de regla venerada
> Que un tiempo en Monserrate apareciera
> De refulgente aureola iluminada
> Sobre radiante disco placentera:
> Por aquella tu esposa idolatrada
> Que en tu seno divino te tuviera,
> Tiende, Señor, el iris de bonanza
> Y al monstruo horrendo en el abismo lanza...
>   Mas si cuadra a tu suma Omnipotencia
> Que yo perezca cual malvado impío,
> Y que los hombres mi cadáver frío
> Ultrajen con maligna complacencia...
> Suene tu voz, y acabe mi existencia...
> Cúmplase en mí tu voluntad, ¡Dios mío!   (pp. 666-667)

For the sake of completing this series of nineteenth-century translations, whose paternity in some cases is rather mysterious, and of proving the poem's popularity in the United States, a fourth version, that published in Brown's *The Black Man*, is included. Of course it appeared too late, 1863, to have influenced Hurlbert:

TO GOD—A PRAYER

> Almighty God! whose goodness knows no bound,
>   To thee I flee in my severe distress;
>   O let thy potent arm my wrongs redress,
> And rend the odious veil by slander wound
> About my brow. The base world's arm confound,
>   Who on my front would now the seal of shame impress.
>
> God of my sires, to whom all kings must yield,
>   Be thou alone my shield; protect me now:
>   All power is His; to whom the sea doth owe
> His countless stores; who clothed with light heaven's field,
> And made the sun, and air, and polar seas congealed;
>   All plants with life endowed, and made the rivers flow.
>
> All power is thine: 'twas thy creative might
>   This goodly frame of things from chaos brought,
>   Which unsustained by thee would still be nought,

As erst it lay deep in the womb of night,
Ere thy dread word first called it into light;
   Obedient to thy call, it lived, and moved, and thought.

Thou know'st my heart, O God, supremely wise;
   Thine eye, all-seeing, cannot be deceived;
   By thee mine inmost soul is clear perceived,
As objects gross are through transparent skies
By mortal ken. Thy mercy exercise,
   Lest slander foul exult o'er innocence aggrieved.

But if 'tis fixed, by thy decree divine,
   That I must bear the pain of guilt and shame,
   And that my foes this cold and senseless frame
Shall rudely treat with scorn and shouts malign,
Give thou the word, and I my breath resign,
   Obedient to thy will. Blest by thy holy name!   (pp. 89-90)

Plácido's second most widely reproduced poem in the United States was "Despedida a mi madre," Morales' version of which follows. Its popularity was due probably to the fact that it, too, was composed in the death house and had the additional emotional appeal of being addressed to the poet's mother:

     Si la suerte fatal que me ha cabido
Y el triste fin de mi sangrienta historia
Al salir de esta vida transitoria
Deja tu corazón de muerte herido,
   Basta de llanto; el ánimo afligido
Recobre su quietud; moro en la gloria,
Y mi plácida lira a tu memoria
Lanza en la tumba su postrer sonido.
   Sonido dulce, melodioso, santo,
Glorioso, espiritual, puro, divino.
Inocente, espontáneo, como el llanto
   Que vertiera al nacer ... ya el cuello inclino,
Ya de la Religión me cubre el manto...
¡Adiós, mi Madre! ¡adiós!—El peregrino.   (p. 37)

Again the English version which became standard was Hurlbert's, which he published in "The Poetry of Spanish America" (p. 148) and in *Gan-Eden* (p. 214):

FAREWELL TO MY MOTHER

> The appointed lot has come upon me, mother,
> The mournful ending of my years of strife;
> This changing world I leave, and to another,
> In blood and terror, goes my spirit's life.
> But thou, grief-smitten, cease thy mortal weeping,
> And let thy soul her wonted peace regain;
> I fall for right, and thoughts of thee are sweeping
> Across my lyre, to wake its dying strain,—
> A strain of joy and gladness, free, unfailing,
> All-glorious and holy, pure, divine,
> And innocent, unconscious as the wailing
> I uttered at my birth; and I resign,
> Even now, my life; even now, descending slowly,
> Faith's mantle folds me to my slumbers holy,
> Mother, farewell! God keep thee, and for ever!

As with the "Plegaria" foreign and North American critics have insisted on attributing the work to a more celebrated Hispanist, in this case William Cullen Bryant. For Hurlbert's translation, Calcagno gives the credit to Bryant and adds that Longfellow prepared a version, too (p. 23n). Bar-Lewaw offers the same information and adds that Bryant's translation is superior to Longfellow's.[81] In *Gems of Spanish Poetry*, Vingut again indicates merely the "N. A. Review" (p. 119). Among the North Americans, it is James Weldon Johnson, in *The Book of American Negro Poetry* (New York, 1922), who revives this misattribution to Byrant (pp. xxxvii, 206).

As did Calcagno before him, Johnson objects to "Bryant's" interpretation of the poem. Johnson points out that "Bryant," probably unaware of Plácido's background, presented a "tender and loving farewell of a son who is about to die to heart-broken mother," whereas, as an abandoned, illegitimate child, Plácido merely "tells her in his last words that he dies happily and bids her not to weep. This he does with nobility and dignity, but absolutely without affection" (pp. xxxvii-xxxviii). Johnson and Calcagno believe the misinterpretation lies with the initial word

---

[81] *Plácido, vida y obra* (Mexico, 1960), pp. 157-159.

Si, omitted by "Bryant," which places the author's grief on a purely hypothetical basis. Johnson then offers what he considers a more accurate translation.

In his article and in *Gan-Eden,* Hurlbert included translations of less well-known examples of Plácido's verse, such as the following "A Grecia." He acknowledged that he secured the Spanish originals from *Isla de Cuba* (Madrid, 1840), by the celebrated Spanish traveler, Jacinto Salas y Quiroga, a great admirer of Plácido. A condensation in Spanish of this traveler's study of the poet, in which are quoted bits of verse and analyses of them, is found in another unidentified clipping in the Wurdemann scrapbook utilized by Hurlbert; probably Hurlbert consulted this condensation rather than the travel book itself. Most of these poems are of a patriotic, anti-Peninsular nature which would have appealed to readers in the United States still aware of their own struggle against Old World domination:

SONNET TO GREECE

Like waves upon the ocean's fitful deep
Is Liberty, rolling her billows o'er
One favored land, while another shore
Her ebbing waters backward slowly creep.
Greece once held wisdom to her fostering breast;
Her Alexander died; a feebler race
Saw the fierce Turk her arts and laws efface,—
The land of gods by godless men oppressed!
She comes again to fill the historian's page.
But, while from Navarino's sands her eyes
See, eddying round the Othman navies, rise
The flames symbolic of her glorious age,
If Greece renews her old triumphant strains,
Unhappy Poland waits to wear her broken chains.

(*NAR,* p. 152)

Como las olas de la mar sombría
Tal es la libertad, pues por un lado
Un pueblo cubre, y deja abandonado
Otro pueblo a la horrenda tiranía.
  Grecia fue centro del saber un día,
Muerto Alejandro, el griego degradado
Vio el país de los dioses subyugado,
Y del turco sufrió la ley impía.

> Tornó a llenar su página en la historia;
> Y si de Navarino en las arenas,
> Al ver las llamas, símbolo de gloria
> Que abrasan las naves sarracenas,
> Cantó la Grecia el himno de victoria,
> Pasaron a Polonia sus cadenas. (*Morales*, p. 33)

Hurlbert translated Salas' introduction to and sample of "La sombra de Padilla," already cited in Spanish as an example of Plácido's political verse of 1834:

> It is truly wonderful to hear a poet, esteemed humble by the society in which he lives, addressing himself to the Queen Regent of Spain in language like this:—
> Some one there is, who, with his golden lyre,
> Worthier thy sovereign ear, shall chant
> To the vibrations of its jewelled strings
> More grateful songs, perchance, but not more free!
> (*NAR*, p. 149)

Next Hurlbert translated stanzas Salas selected from Plácido's "La profecía de Cuba a España, en los días de D.ª Isabel de Borbón" and Salas' remark, "and these lines are equally bold and daring." Curiously enough, the last four lines of Salas' version, and consequently of Hurlbert's English one, do not appear in Morales':

> And beats not thy heart, too? Therefore will I,
> While the pure dawn her snowy canopy
>   Hangs on the orient sky,
> Bid my rejoicing hymns to God on high,
> Upborne by gentlest breezes, swiftly fly:—
> Let them who fear be dumb, for not of them am I!
> If thou with pleasure hearest, let thy prayers
> Swift seek the Eternal, that my songs may rise
> Even to his throne, and then on Cuba fall,
> Impearled in blessings from the echoing skies!
> (*NAR*, pp. 149-150)

> ¿El corazón no os late? Pues en tanto
> Que adorna el firmamento
> El alba pura con nevado manto
> Himnos de gozo sobre el leve viento
> A la región olímpica levanto:
> Calle el que tema: yo no temo y canto.
> (*Morales*, p. 654)

Then follows Hurlbert's translation of Salas' sample of "Al cumpleaños de S. M. la Reina Gobernadora," with accompanying comments:

> In a country where the faintest idea of a liberal tendency is sternly repressed, where the singers of the opera were obliged to change the word 'Liberty,' whenever it occurred in an Italian *libretto*, into the word 'Loyalty,' the government permitted the publication of such verses as these:—
>> Hail, Liberty! a thousand times all hail!
>> For that, propitious, on thine every path
>> Thou scatterest, with placid influence,
>> The seeds beneficent of science,
>> Of peace, of plenty, and of justice!
>>> (*NAR*, p. 150)

> Salud ¡oh libertad! salud mil veces,
> Pues derramas propicia
> Do quier que vas, con plácida influencia,
> El benéfico germen de la ciencia,
> La abundancia, la paz y la justicia.
>> (*Poesías de Plácido* [Paris, 1862], pp. 102-103)

Hurlbert continued as follows with his translation of Salas' selection of bits of verse and comments:

> Almost all the versification of this poet is of this manly nature; his sonnets to Napoleon, to Christ, and to William Tell, are three jewels of our literature; the conclusion of the last is a noble cry of indignation:—
>> That even the insensate elements
>> Fling back the despot's ashes from their breasts.
>>> (*NAR*, p. 150)

MUERTE DE GESSLER

> Y hasta los insensibles elementos
> Lanzan de sí los restos de un tirano.
>> (*Morales*, p. 32)

As the last translation, Hurlbert included "Hymn to Liberty," of which he said: "For this spirited translation we are indebted to an anonymous writer in the New York Tribune" (*NAR*, p. 153*n*). An undated clipping in the Wurdemann scrapbook proves that such a "translation," signed "Humanity," did appear in print. Its author claimed that is was a translation of one of Plácido's poems composed during his final imprisonment, but it resembles none of the known works, either the early or late works. It seems that "Humanity" played a trick on the conscientious Hurlbert.

In addition to the English versions of Salas' selections, Hurlbert included one stanza from "En la proclamación de Isabel II, Reina de España," and left it in Spanish as Salas had reproduced it:

> De gozo enajenados mis sentidos,
> Fijé mi vista en las serenas ondas,
> Y vi las ninfas revolver gallardas
> Las rubias hebras de sus Arenzas blondas.
>   (*NAR*, p. 150)

With her fantastic account of Plácido's life, Barr included a translation. It, like her biographical data, belongs to Manzano, not to Plácido. The two stanzas she selected are the first and last of the eight-stanza poem "Ode to Religion," published in *Poems by a Slave in the Island of Cuba* (pp. 98-100). Apparently Mrs. Barr appropriated the translation as well as the biography, without any acknowledgment, from Richard Robert Madden.

Since North American interest in Plácido seems to have subsided at the turn of the century, very few English translations have been composed in this century. The reworking of the *Despedida* by Johnson, the anthologist of Negro poetry, is one of the few, and Carruthers includes some of his own in his dissertation. Especially interesting are those—including yet another version of the "Plegaria"—to be found in the article "Gabriel de la Concepción Valdés: His Life and His Works," *Inter-America*, VIII (New York, 1924), 152-165. This is the English version (translator unidentified) of the speech which Emilia Bernal delivered at the Sorbonne, December 10, 1923, and which was first published as "Los poetas mártires, Gabriel de la Concepción Valdés: su vida y su obra," in *Cuba Contemporánea*, XXXV (Habana, 1924), 216-232.

Chapter IV

CONCLUSION

In an effort to judge Plácido as a person, by putting together the pieces of the jigsaw puzzle left by biographies and documents, one can arrive at fairly definite conclusions only about his appearance. Despite the debate over portraits and the size of his eyes, he was handsome and light of skin. Reports of his character are conflicting. From the standpoint of morals, these reports range from eulogies of his clean living and integrity to diatribes about his dissoluteness and, at the time of the trial, his betrayal of companions. From the standpoint of leadership ability and social and political awareness, they run the gamut from the theory that he was a timid, fawning mulatto, a scatter-brained "true poet," to the theory that he was a clever undercover agent, a strong-willed reformer who went unerringly to his goal. With regard to his education, some maintain that he was almost illiterate, and others say that he was wonderfully well self-taught.

Today, in reassessing his character in light of some new material, one might approximate the truth most closely by taking a middle road with respect to these extremes. And it would seem safe to correct the biographers on at least one score—that of Plácido's emotional tie to his mother. Apparently he loved her more than most critics (understandably, considering that she abandoned him at birth) have realized. Perhaps this love was harmful, for Concepción's failure to demonstrate publicly her affection and support must have affected the youth more than if their relationship had been indifferent. Assuming an Oedipus complex, complicated by this outwardly, at least, unrequited love, one might make of Plácido a critical psychopathic case.

Everything seems to lead to the conclusion that, if not emotionally crippled, at least he was far more tormented and maladjusted than has been previously imagined. The fact that biographers agree scarcely on a single facet of his personality may indicate that this personality was, at best, mercurial. Evidences of his lack of stability are many; they include his inability to manage his financial affairs, his constant lending and borrowing, his strange disappearances lasting weeks at a time, and the wild sensuality possibly indicated by certain of his verses, a sensuality that he must have had no trouble gratifying, favored as he was with good looks and placed in a tropical environment offering opportunities for all manner of sexual indulgence. Of course, most striking of all evidences of instability was his avoidance, despite this sexual prowess, of lasting attachments with women other than his mother, while, at the same time, he formed lifetime friendships with older men, often his employers.

Perhaps the most important question is whether Plácido was capable of plotting and participating in an insurrection directed against either the white race or against Spanish despots. With the type of temperament suggested above, it would seem that he was not; yet, paradoxically, the documents which have appeared in the twentieth century prove fairly conclusively that he was indeed involved, that he was cunning and so closemouthed as to keep the certainty of his involvement a secret for over a century.

Many factors account for the difficulty in securing more data and in interpreting what is available. For instance, out of fear of reprisals by the Spanish government, many owners must have destroyed their documents. Furthermore, not only the authors of the fictionized treatments, but some biographers as well, especially Morales, converted Plácido's character into that "del tipo imaginado, del tipo legendario, del personaje de novela, del protagonista de drama romántico"—to use the words of Figarola-Caneda, who disapproved of this tendency (p. 193). Thus the poet's personality has been obscured. Bachiller y Morales believed that Plácido was not the leader of the *Conspiración*, nor was he "un héroe de leyenda," but he was a "gran poeta como lo reconoce hoy el mundo literario y como pasará a la posteridad." [82]

This tendency to romanticize Plácido's life is quite understandable. Although his wretched social position cannot be termed "romantic" in the general sense of the word, in the literary sense it might be so classified — to a degree, at least. For example, like the hero of one of the most typically romantic of Spanish dramas, *Don Álvaro, o La fuerza del sino*, Plácido died young, an outcast from society through no fault of his own. Like Don Álvaro, he was the offspring of the New World and of mixed blood; in the case of the fictitious hero, of course, the socially unacceptable drop was Indian. Presumably both young men were handsome and noble in bearing. Some might see also in Plácido a touch of the Don Juanesque, a characteristic associated with the type of romantic hero as portrayed on the stage by Zorrilla. Furthermore, writing poetry was the proper occupation for a Byronic hero, especially if it was romantic poetry, as Plácido's often was.

Perhaps Plácido should be classified as an heroic figure rather than a romantic one. He was heroic in that he managed to rise above his station in life: "Interesante, patético, admirable es la vida del hombre que, sujeto a un medio determinado y cohibido por él, se sobrepone a él, y se eleva por su propio esfuerzo, y se purifica por la acción espontánea de su conciencia. Desde este punto de vista, la vida de Plácido es admirable. Fue débil porque el medio en que vivió lo oprimía; fue fuerte porque triunfó del medio opresor." [83]

From even a summary study of Cuban poetry, it becomes obvious that much of it was a poetry of political movements which were closely connected to movements in the United States. To interpret the conflicting biographical data concerning Plácido, it seems advisable to study him from the vantage point not only of his Cuban contemporaries but of those in the United States. It will be found that although the abolitionist group tended to romanticize him, one member, Hurlbert, wrote a most creditable

---

[82] *Revista Cubana*, I (Havana, 1885), 547.
[83] Hostos, p. 24.

biography, and another Carolinian, Wurdemann, may have contributed some facts which even Cuban scholars failed to uncover.

In general it was Plácido's life, not his poetry, which captured the attention of his northern audience. His life was passed in a glamorous setting and during an exciting period in history. Cuba's political relations with the United States were making headlines, and the *affaire Escalera* furnished abolitionists with fuel for their fire. The psychological reasons why the United States took such an interest in Plácido are summed up in the preface to the mysterious "Hymn to Liberty," published in the *Tribune* and preserved in the Wurdemann scrapbook. In this passage, in which the righteously indignant author objects to apparently pro-slavery feelings of a certain "Scabolo," it is the romantic figure of a "Patriot and Martyr" that really fascinates the author; as an afterthought, the poetry is mentioned:

> A communication lately appeared in the New-York Sun, touching the Cuban Negro Poet Placido, and which alludes to him in a manner that betrays either an ignorance of his character or a determination to make him infamous, simply because the attempted revolution which lost him his life interferes with the political schemes or "peculiar institution" notions of the writer. Placido was the head of an organization at Matanzas and elsewhere, on the Island of Cuba, having for its object freedom from Slavery for the black of that Island. It was not an organization against *taxes*, as in the Revolution of '76, so much vaunted — but against actual fetters and whips, whose marks and scars might be traced on every plantation; and yet this "Scabolo" of the New-York Sun (God grant he is not an American, or a *man*) calls the attempted revolution for the freedom of some millions of horribly bonded human beings as "atrocious conspiracy." I should like to see "Scabolo" under the full enjoyment of that *regime* which roused the noble-souled Placido, — then, perhaps, the principles of American Liberty might inspire a different estimate. Placido was a patriot and a holy martyr. He was actuated by the highest influences that ever inspired humanity to resist oppression. He met his death and all the scoffs and tortures which the inquisitorials of Spain could inflict, without yielding a point or betraying an accomplice. Cuba has few such men: if she had, all her bonds would have been cast deep into the Gulf long

ago. Placido was a true Poet, too, as well as Patriot and Martyr; and the soul that is exalted by true poetry has such cognizance of God that it scorns human bondage.

In romanticizing Plácido's life, there lies the danger not only of losing sight of his true character, but of allowing admiration of his heroism to enhance the quality of his verse. The poet does not need these odds, for as even the celebrated Peninsular critic, Menéndez y Pelayo, admits, Plácido's worth stems from more than pity; some of his poetry ranks with the very best produced in Spanish America: "Quien escribió el magistral y primoroso romance de *Xicotencal*, que Góngora no desdeñaría entre los suyos, el bello soneto descriptivo *La Muerte de Gessler*, la graciosa letrilla de *La Flor de la caña* y la inspirada plegaria que iba recitando camino del patíbulo, no necesita ser mulato ni haber sido fusilado para que la posteridad se acuerde de él." [84]

In reassessing Plácido as a poet, he emerges, historically at least, as a far more significant figure than critics have ever realized. Since "la Avellaneda" really belonged to Spain rather than to Cuba, since Heredia is basically neo-classic, and since critics are now classifying Martí as a Modernist, it would seem that Plácido was Cuba's outstanding romantic poet. Perhaps he was one of the leading romanticists not only of Cuba, but of all Spanish America, because he helped to initiate trends which later in the century were to become characteristic of the work of the most famous of the romanticists in the Spanish New World, those of Argentina. He wrote verse extolling political liberalism, and, as early as or earlier than Esteban Echeverría, for instance, he was exalting indigenous heroes and turning to his own country for inspiration, instead of to lands remote in time and space. Thus he was also an important precursor of the *siboneístas*, whom Cubans like to think are uniquely Cuban, but who are simply romanticists glorifying their own Island.

In all fairness, however, it should be noted that, although much of Plácido's verse deals with political freedom, essentially he was not a political poet. Foremost he was a poet of occasion and of the exotic and fanciful. It is in this particular type of romanticism, as

---

[84] *Antología de poetas hispano-americanos* (Madrid, 1927), II, xxxv.

illustrated by "La flor de la caña," where his originality and inherent genius appear and where he shows himself to be ahead of his times:

>Yo vi una veguera
>Trigueña tostada,
>Que el sol, envidioso
>De sus lindas gracias,
>O quizá bajando
>De su esfera sacra,
>Prendado de ella
>Le quemó la cara.
>Y es tierna y modesta
>Cuando saca sus primeros tilos
>"La flor de la caña"... (p. 430)

To analyze Plácido's poetry, as well as his life, it is worthwhile to look to the United States. The English translations may throw some light on the originals, as in the case of Hurlbert's and Morales' versions of the "Plegaria." And in the process of studying the material in English, various erroneous attributions to famous North American translators and Hispanists and other mistakes on the part of critics in the North and in Cuba may be corrected; likewise, incorrect attributions to Plácido of Manzano's poetry and faulty information about Cuba may be set right.

Plácido's "blossom poems" and *siboney* verse are aesthetically superior to his "prison poems," which are primarily of historical and biographical importance. Furthermore, there is no question about the authenticity of the former group of works, while doubt still lingers concerning the paternity of the second group. But indisputable is the fact that Plácido's fame — not only in the United States of the nineteenth century, but in the Spanish world — has rested on what are considered his last five compositions.

The doubts raised by Sanguily and other critics, such as Piñeyro, considering their authorship — in particular the authorship of the "Plegaria" — were partially quelled by Francisco González del Valle, in ¿*Es de Plácido la Plegaria a Dios?* (Havana, 1923), and by the summary of this study included in the biography by Garófalo Mesa (pp. 207-227). It has been pointed out that Plácido's verse composed in the Trinidad prison gives proof of his ability to write under duress; if critics ceased insisting that three of the poems were created during the last twenty-four hours of his five-month imprisonment in Matanzas, it could be said that he had sufficient time in which to compose the five famous works. The problem of how they passed from prison to print does not seem insurmountable. Since they contain very little political propaganda, they could easily have been removed from his cell by friends, such as Morales or the priest García; Horrego Estuch believes that Plácido entrusted them to his wife ([1960], p. 238). The fact that they were first printed in Spain, not in Cuba, might seem logical, since the local government would certainly have suppressed any attempt to publish such poetry. And none of Plácido's contemporaries ever rose to claim them.

Perhaps the most conclusive proof of the paternity of the "Plegaria" is the careful collation by González del Valle of figures of speech used in this poem and in other of Plácido's works; few of these expressions are unique to the "Plegaria." The same critic adds that any other poet would have been so moved to indignation by the thoughts of the unjust execution that he would have filled this serene poem with bitterness and harsh attacks against the authorities.

Some of the arguments in favor of Plácido's authorship of the "Plegaria" and the other four poems are not convincing. Naturally none of the poet's contemporaries in Cuba rose to claim them, just as no Cuban newspaper dared to print them. Even the proof of repeated figures of speech is not completely conclusive, for any talented writer familiar with Plácido's verse could have collected the poet's favorite expressions and worked them into the "Plegaria." No one has attempted to explain other possible evidences of spuriousness. The mystery of why Zambrana maintained that Plácido recited "A la fatalidad," not the "Plegaria," on his death march has never been cleared up. Disconcerting, too, is the question as to how the poems reached Spain so quickly.

A strong suspicion must still remain that an ardent abolitionist or disgruntled Cuban refugee — probably living in Madrid, since the poems first appeared there — composed and published them under Plácido's name, in order to attract universal sympathy for the causes that Cuban poet symbolized. It is to be regretted that Plácido's fame has not resulted from his less pretentious and more delicate poems dealing with Cuba's customs and scenery.

A SELECTED BIBLIOGRAPHY

BIOGRAPHIES AND ANTHOLOGIES IN SPANISH

BACHILLER Y MORALES, ANTONIO. "Plácido," *Revista Cubana*, II (Havana, 1885), 547-561.
BAR-LEWAW, ITZHAK. *Plácido, vida y obra*. Mexico, 1960.
BERNAL, EMILIA. "Los poetas mártires, Gabriel de la Concepción Valdés: su vida y su obra," *Cuba Contemporánea*, XXXV (Havana, 1924), 216-232.
BRAVO, EMILIO. "Literatura española en Cuba," *Semanario Pintoresco Español*, Madrid, 1849, pp. 348-349, 366-367.
CALCAGNO, FRANCISCO. *Diccionario biográfico cubano*. New York, 1878.
———. *Poetas de color*. Havana, 1878.
CASALS, JORGE. *Plácido como poeta cubano*. Havana, 1944.
CORONADO, FRANCISCO P. DE. "Centenario de Plácido," *La Discusión*, Havana, March 20, 1909, pp. 9, 12.
Evolución de la cultura cubana, 1608-1927. Vol. II, *La poesía lírica en Cuba*. Edited by José Manuel Carbonell y Rivero. Havana, 1928.
FIGAROLA-CANEDA, DOMINGO. *Plácido (poeta cubano)*. Havana, 1922.
F. U. "Plácido el mulato," *Revista de Teatros*, Madrid, September 20, 23, 26, 30, 1844, no page numbers.
GARÓFALO MESA, GARCÍA. *Plácido, poeta y mártir*. Mexico, 1938.
GUITERAS, PEDRO JOSÉ. "Estudios de literatura cubana, Gabriel de la Concepción Valdés," *El Mundo Nuevo*, New York, January 1, 1874, p. 6; January 15, pp. 22-23; February 1, p. 42.
HORREGO ESTUCH, LEOPOLDO. *Plácido, el poeta infortunado*. Havana, 1944.
———. ———. 2d ed. Havana, 1949.
———. ———. Havana, 1960.
HOSTOS, EUGENIO MARÍA DE. *Obras completas*. Vol IX, *Temas cubanos*, Havana, 1939.
PIÑEYRO, ENRIQUE. "Gabriel de la Concepción Valdés." In *Biografías americanas*. Paris, 1906.
RIVERA, GUILLERMO. "El ensayo de Hostos sobre Plácido," *Hispania*, XXII (1939), 145-152.
TRELLES, CARLOS M. *Biografía cubana del siglo XIX*, Vol. II. Matanzas, 1912.
VALDÉS, GABRIEL DE LA CONCEPCIÓN. *Plácido (Gabriel de la Concepción Valdés) Poesías completas*. Con... un prólogo biográfico por Sebastián Alfredo de Morales. Havana, 1886.
———. *Poesías selectas de Plácido*. Introducción por A. M. Eligio de la Puente. Havana, 1930.

———. *Poésies complètes de Placido*. Traduites par D. Fontaine avec préface de Louis Jourdan. Paris, 1863.

UNPUBLISHED LETTERS AND MISCELLANY

Escoto, José A. "Plácido Material." Box 17, Bundle III, SAL 475.1.2. Harvard University Library.
Hurlbert, William H. "William M. Evarts Papers," Vols. 11, 15, 20-21, 23-27. The Library of Congress.
———. "William Collins Whitney Papers," Vols. 15-17. The Library of Congress.
Wurdemann, J. G. F. "Poems of Gabriel de la Concepción Valdés." SAL 475.1.2. Harvard University Library.
———. "Miscellaneous Papers (Wurdemann Folder)." Manuscript Division, The New York Public Library.

OUTSTANDING EDITIONS

Poesías de Plácido. Matanzas: Imprenta de Gobierno y Marina, 1838.
El Veguero. Matanzas: Imprenta de Comercio, 1841.
Poesías escojidas de Plácido. Matanzas: Imprenta de Gobierno, 1842.
El hijo de maldición. Matanzas: Imprenta de Gobierno, 1843.
Poesías de Plácido. New York: Roe, Lockwood & Son, 1854.
Poesías de Plácido. New York: Roe, Lockwood & Son, 1855.
Poesías completas de Plácido. Mexico: En casa de Mme C. Denné Schmitz, 1856.
Poesías de Plácido. 2 vols. New York: Roe Lockwood & Son, 1857.
Poesías completas de Plácido. Paris: En casa de Mme C. Denné Schmitz, 1857.
Poesías completas de Plácido. 3d ed. Paris: Librería española de Mme C. Schmitz e hijo, 1862.

CONSPIRACIÓN DE LA ESCALERA

Blanchet, Emilio. "El fusilamiento de Plácido," *El Álbum* (número extraordinario en obsequio de Plácido), Matanzas, June 28, 1904, no page numbers.
La Comisión Militar Ejecutiva y Permanente de la Isla de Cuba. Discurso leído por el académico de número Capitán Joaquín Llaverías en la sesión solemne celebrada el 10 de octubre de 1929. Havana: Academia de la Historia de Cuba, 1929.
De Acevedo, Roberto P., and Alonso y Artigas, Benito. "Nuevas noticias y documentos acerca del poeta Plácido," *El País*, Havana, January 25, 1941, p. 12.
González del Valle, Francisco. *La conspiración de la escalera*. Vol. I, *José de la Luz y Caballero*. Havana, 1925.
Márquez, José de Jesús. *Plácido y los conspiradores de 1844*. Havana, 1894.
Morales y Morales, Vidal. *Iniciadores y primeros mártires de la revolución*

cubana. Con introducción por Fernando Ortiz y biografía por Rafael Montoro, Vol. I. Havana, 1931.

Publicaciones del Archivo Nacional de Cuba. Vol. III, *Catálogo de los fondos de la Comisión Militar Ejecutiva y Permanente de la Isla de Cuba.* Havana, 1945.

RODRÍGUEZ, JOSÉ IGNACIO. *Vida de don José de la Luz y Caballero.* New York, 1879.

VARONA, ENRIQUE JOSÉ. "El caso de Mr. Turnbull." In Saco, José Antonio. *Historia de la esclavitud de la raza africana en el nuevo mundo y en especial en los países américo-hispanos,* Vol. IV. Havana, 1938.

STYLISTIC STUDIES

Antología de poetas hispano-americanos. Vol. II, *Cuba, Santo Domingo, Puerto Rico, Venezuela.* Introducción por M. Menéndez y Pelayo. Madrid, 1927.

CARILLA, EMILIO. *El romanticismo en la América Hispánica.* Madrid, 1958.

FEIJÓO, SAMUEL. "Sobre los movimientos por una poesía cubana hasta 1856," *Revista Cubana,* XXV (Havana, 1949), 64-176.

GONZÁLEZ DEL VALLE, FRANCISCO. *¿Es de Plácido la Plegaria a Dios? Discurso de recepción leído ante la Academia de la Historia el 16 de julio de 1923.* Havana, 1923.

LASO DE LOS VÉLEZ, PEDRO. *Plácido, su biografía, juicio crítico y análisis de sus más escogidas poesías.* Barcelona, 1875.

MENÉNDEZ Y PELAYO, MARCELINO. *Horacio en España,* Vol. II. Madrid, 1885.

MITJANS, AURELIO. *Estudio sobre el movimiento científico y literario de Cuba.* Havana, 1890.

REMOS Y RUBIO, JUAN J. *Historia de la literatura cubana.* Vol. II, *Romanticismo.* Havana, 1945.

SAIZ DE LA MORA, JESÚS. *Plácido, su popularidad, su obra, y sus críticos, en el 75° aniversario de su muerte.* Havana, 1919.

SANGUILY, MANUEL. "Un improvisador cubano" and "Otra vez Plácido y Menéndez Pelayo," *Hojas Literarias,* III (Havana, 1894), 93-121, 227-269.

VITIER, CINTIO. *Lo cubano en la poesía.* Havana, 1958.

NORTH AMERICAN BIOGRAPHIES AND TRANSLATIONS

ANON. "[Plácido]," *The Harbinger,* IV (Boston, 1847), 321-323.

BARR, AMELIA E. "Plácido: Slave, Poet, and Martyr," *The Christian Union,* VIII (New York, 1873), 62-63.

BERNAL, EMILIA. "Gabriel de la Concepción Valdés: His Life and His Work," *Inter-America,* VIII (New York, 1924), 152-165.

BROWN, WILLIAM WELLS. *The Black Man, His Antecedents, His Genius, and His Achievements.* New York, 1863.

CARRUTHERS, BEN FREDERIC. "The Life, Work and Death of Plácido," Unpublished Ph. D. dissertation, University of Illinois, 1941.

The Catholic Anthology. Edited by Thomas Walsh. New York, 1939.

CHAPMAN, MARIA WESTON. "Placido," *The Liberty Bell,* Boston, 1845, pp. 67-71.

Coester, Alfred. *The Literary History of Spanish America*. 2d ed. New York, 1938.
Everett, Alexander H. "Havana." In *Critical and Miscellaneous Essays*. 2d series. Boston, 1846, pp. 325-380.
[———.] "La Havane," *Southern Quarterly Review*, VII (Charleston, 1845), 153-196.
Gems of Spanish Poetry. Edited by Francisco Javier Vingut. New York, 1855.
Hispanic Anthology. Edited by Thomas Walsh. New York, 1920.
[Hurlbert, William H.] "The Poetry of Spanish America," *The North American Review*, LXVIII (Boston, 1849), 129-160.
Johnson, James Weldon. *The Book of American Negro Poetry*. New York, 1922.
Leavitt, Sturgis E. *Hispano-American Literature in the United States*. Cambridge, Mass., 1932.
———. "Latin-American Literature in the United States," *Revue de Littérature comparée*, XI (1931), 126-148.
Stimson, Frederick S. *Orígenes del hispanismo norteamericano*. Mexico, 1961.
———. "Una poesía desconocida de Plácido," *Revista Iberoamericana*, XXIV (1959), 363-366.
——— and Bininger, Robert J. "Studies of Bryant as Hispanophile: Another Translation," *American Literature*, XXXI (1959), 189-191.

NINETEENTH-CENTURY TRAVEL LITERATURE PERTAINING TO CUBA

Bryant, William C. *Prose Writings of William Cullen Bryant*. Edited by Parke Godwin. 2 vols. New York, 1884.
———. *Letters of a Traveller*. London, 1850.
Dana, Jr., Richard Henry. *To Cuba and Back*. Boston, 1859.
Davey, Richard. *Cuba Past and Present*. London, 1898.
Davis, Richard Harding. *Cuba in War Time*. New York, 1899.
Humboldt, Alexander. *The Island of Cuba*. Translated by J. S. Thrasher. New York, 1856.
Hurlbert, William H. *Gan-Eden: or, Pictures of Cuba*. Boston, 1854.
———. *Pictures of Cuba*. London, 1855.
Madden, Richard Robert. *The Island of Cuba*. London, 1849.
Merlín, María de las Mercedes. *La Havane*. 3 vols. Paris, 1844.
Rowan, Andrew Summers, and Ramsey, Marathon Montrose. *The Island of Cuba*. New York, 1896.
Salas y Quiroga, Jacinto. *Viages de D. Jacinto de Salas y Quiroga*. Vol. I, *Isla de Cuba*. Madrid, 1840.
Smith, Aaron. *The Atrocities of the Pirates; being a faithful narrative of the unparalleled sufferings endured by the author during his captivity among the pirates of the Island of Cuba*. 2d ed. London, 1929.
Turnbull, David. *Travels in the West. Cuba; with Notices of Porto Rico and the Slave Trade*. London, 1840.
Wurdemann, J. G. F. *Notes on Cuba, Containing an Account of its Discovery and Early History; a Description of the Face of the Country; its Population, Resources and Wealth; its Institutions, and the Manners and Customs of its Inhabitants*. Boston, 1844.

MISCELLANEOUS

Aureola poética a Don Francisco Martínez de la Rosa por las musas del Almendares. Havana, 1834.

CHAPMAN, CHARLES E. *A History of the Cuban Republic.* New York, 1927.

GUZMÁN, AUGUSTO. *Historia de la novela boliviana.* La Paz, Bolivia, 1938.

MANZANO, JUAN FRANCISCO. *Poems by a Slave in the Island of Cuba.* Translated by R. R. Madden. London, 1840.

MOTT, FRANK LUTHER. *A History of American Magazines.* Vol. I, 1741-1850. New York, 1930. Vol. II, *1850-1865*. Cambridge, Mass., 1938.

SAGRA, RAMÓN DE LA. *Historia económico-política y estadística de la Isla de Cuba.* Havana, 1831.

TEJERA, DIEGO VICENTE. *La muerte de Plácido.* New York, 1875.

VILLA, JOSÉ G. "Gabriel de la Concepción Valdés," *El Tipógrafo*, Matanzas, January 26, 1902, p. 1.

VILLAVERDE, CIRILO. "La peineta calada," *Faro Industrial de la Habana,* Havana, February-March, 1843.

WILLIAMS, STANLEY T. *The Spanish Background of American Literature.* 2 vols. New Haven, 1955.

www.ingramcontent.com/pod-product-compliance
Lightning Source LLC
Chambersburg PA
CBHW021845220426
43663CB00005B/414